THE ART OF INBOUND MARKETING

2.0:

REVISED AND UPDATED

THE HOW-TO GUIDE FOR FINANCIAL ADVISORS

CRAIG J. FAULKNER | CEO, FMG SUITE

Copyright © 2017

ISBN: 978-1-5323-1940-2

First Edition

All rights reserved. Printed in China. No part of this book may be reproduced or transmitted in any form or by any means, electronic or mechanical, including photocopying, recording, or by an information storage and retrieval system — except by a reviewer who may quote brief passages in a review to be printed in a magazine or newspaper — without permission in writing from the publisher.

ACKNOWLEDGEMENTS

MARILYN GREEN FAULKNER

This book has been a joint project with my wife, Marilyn. My collaboration with Marilyn began thirty years ago when we created The Complete Financial Management Workshop™, the first comprehensive seminar system for financial advisors. I was the "idea guy," and knew how to create a visual, polished product. Marilyn could capture it in writing in a compelling style. This has worked for us ever since.

This book has followed the same pattern. I talk, Marilyn writes, and together we come up with something better than either of us could do separately. Our collaboration seems to have worked in other areas as well, resulting in five great kids and nine wonderful grandchildren!

MELISSA DARCEY AND MARINA GRINDLE

As FMG Suite's marketing manager, Melissa helped keep this project on track, from the initial brainstorming sessions to the final printing. And along with our copywriter, Marina, they helped me develop ideas, condense my thoughts, and write and edit what transformed into an amazing second version of *The Art of Inbound Marketing*. This book wouldn't have been possible without the team efforts, marketing insights, and writing and editing talents of Melissa and Marina.

BRANDON BROWN AND HEIDI SAUCIER

A design dream team, FMG Suite's Vice President of Creative, Brandon, and Vice President of Marketing, Heidi, continuously help maintain a strong brand identity both for myself and FMG Suite. The style and aesthetics of this book are the result of their creativity.

ADDITIONAL THANKS

I also want to express sincere appreciation to an outstanding design team: Joe Massey, FMG Suite's own graphic designer, for his outstanding art design for the front and back cover, and Victoria Morgan, who helped us design, format, and layout the manuscript and prepare it for the printer.

TABLE OF CONTENTS

FOREWORD

By Michael Kitces, MSFS, MTAX, CFP, CLU, ChFC
Partner & Director of Wealth Management,
Pinnacle Advisory Group
Co-Founder, XY Planning Network
Publisher, Nerd's Eye View blog, Kitces.com

In 2008, I launched a blog called Nerd's Eye View to share some of my thoughts and commentary in the world of financial planning. I certainly wasn't the first person to ever launch a blog—not by a long shot—but among financial planners I was one of the early adopters of blogging. My reasoning for starting the blog wasn't particularly elaborate or terribly well thought out; it amounted to little more than the fact that blogging seemed to be a popular and effective thing to do in other industries, so there must be some potential in our industry too, right?

Yet, in lacking any idea of what to do, or even having any clear strategy for the blog's business purpose, my efforts didn't seem to be making any progress. There were hardly any comments, there wasn't much engagement, and I felt like I was just spinning my wheels. A look into my site's traffic statistics on Google Analytics after the first six months confirmed my suspicions; the blog had little activity and wasn't growing. So, I simply stopped writing and let it go dormant. For two years.

In the middle of 2010, though, I had what for me was a "light bulb moment"—that instance when inspiration strikes and it suddenly clicks. For me, the epiphany was watching the explosive growth of social media, and in particular, the way that people shared articles with each other on social media. I realized that social media had created a whole new means for people to find and discover content and for it to be seen and shared. I had always known that I had a skill set to create content that would be valuable, but I never knew how I'd get anyone to check it out in the first place. Now I knew; the blog would be the hub for all my content, and social media would be how people found it. And so Nerd's Eye View was reborn.

In the four years since that relaunch, I've had the great fortune of watching my blog explode from my little personal corner of the web where I shared some of my thoughts, to a thriving website that has completely transformed both my career and professional life.

In fact, one of the greatest challenges has been figuring out how to manage all the connections that have been made, all the opportunities that have come forth, and all the businesses that I have spawned as my readership grows. A nice problem to have, for sure, but one I couldn't have even imagined just four years ago.

However, the success of the blog was not without its challenges along the way. The path I was stumbling into, through a slow and painful process of self-discovery and learning by the school of hard knocks, has been dubbed "inbound marketing" in recognition of the concept that marketing doesn't have to be about advertising outbound to people; instead, it can simply be about creating and sharing value and letting people find their way to you.

I didn't know anything about inbound marketing at the time, but it's something I've learned about since, as I eventually figured out that there's a lot of knowledge out there about inbound marketing and how to do it effectively. Unfortunately, though, as I went down the path, there was virtually nothing about it in our world of financial services.

The lack of any good books or information about inbound marketing for financial advisors is a bit of a shock in many ways. After all, the essence of inbound marketing is about demonstrating your expertise to become a recognized expert, and then consistently dripping out content to reinforce your value and skill, until eventually, people are ready to do business with you. That approach is nothing new for financial advisors, who for decades have done public seminars as marketing to demonstrate such expertise, and have published and mailed print newsletters to maintain a drip-marketing campaign with prospective clients. In that context, blogging and social media are really nothing more than the new media platforms for a very old advisor strategy designed to demonstrate expertise, build trust, and grow an advisory business.

Fortunately, this problem of little to no inbound marketing information for financial advisors is slowly being rectified. Articles are now being written about the value of inbound marketing for advisors. Consultants who can help put this strategy into practice are emerging. Tools and software are being developed—or adapted—for financial advisors to use. A new age of inbound marketing for advisors is upon us, where blogging and social media are the new tools of the trade for demonstrating expertise, building trust, and ultimately establishing new client relationships.

It is in this context that, in 2014, I was quite excited to hear that Craig Faulkner had decided to write what, to my knowledge, was the very first standalone book on inbound marketing specifically for financial advisors. Now, he's updated it to a revised version that reflects the latest industry changes and marketing evolutions.

Even several years later, Craig Faulkner's book remains one of the few on the market that tackles the unique challenges of digital and inbound marketing for financial advisors. This is a handbook for the advisor's journey into the new age of marketing and can help advisors understand the importance of blogging and content, how to create value for prospective clients, the role that social media plays, and how to put it all together, with practical tips and best practices along the way.

I wish there had been a book like this when I launched my blog and began my own journey into the world of social media and inbound marketing, to help me understand what I should be doing and to avoid the novice mistakes. I wasn't so lucky, and had to learn the hard way. Fortunately, now you can simply read the book, and get some help to jumpstart your own journey!

Michael Kitces, MSFS, MTAX, CFP, CLU, ChFC
Partner & Director of Wealth Management,
Pinnacle Advisory Group
Co-Founder, XY Planning Network
Publisher, Nerd's Eye View blog, www.kitces.com

INTRODUCTION:

RE-PEELING THE BANANA

I've been in the marketing world for decades, but it wasn't until 2014 that I finally sat down and wrote a book about what I have learned. *The Art of Inbound Marketing* focused specifically on financial advisors. I set out to help advisors understand how marketing has shifted — from a print-based megaphone to a digital magnet — and how they can address these new rules in their main marketing outlets, including websites, social media, email, and presentations.

If you watch FMG Suite's live broadcasts, you may have heard me share the idea-sparking "banana peel story." While discussing his latest recipe for a morning shake, my dad asked me if I knew how to peel a banana. I laughed. "Of course I do! What could be simpler? I suppose over the course of my life I've peeled a few thousand of them."

But my dad just grinned and said, "Then show me!" So we got a couple of bananas from the kitchen and I peeled mine, firmly grabbing it by the stem and tugging until it came apart. My dad smiled and said, "I knew you didn't know how. Let me show you how monkeys peel a banana." To my surprise, rather than tugging on the stem as I had done, he turned the banana upside down and pinched the bottom. The peel split easily and the banana opened like a dream.

Just as my dad taught me a new way to peel a banana (by pinching the bottom), I wanted to show advisors a different way to peel the marketing banana: by turning the banana upside down and looking at marketing through a new lens. Instead of blasting your name out to as many people as possible, inbound marketing is about helping your ideal client base find you, learn from you, talk to you, and trust you.

AN EVER-EVOLVING INDUSTRY

While these rules still apply today, the marketing landscape has shifted again. In just these past two years, the financial services industry has further evolved and, as a result, so must marketing strategies. For example, in 2015 the robo-advisor jumped to the forefront of online investing and financial services. With robo's low investment fees, advisors may need to adjust their messaging to clients to emphasize the importance of advisor–client relationships and personalized advice over costs.

In addition, Millennials surpassed Baby Boomers as the nation's largest living generation in early 2016, becoming advisors' second-largest potential client base.[1] Over the next 40 years, Baby Boomers will transfer $30 trillion to Generation X and Y heirs, meaning advisors will have to adjust their marketing and business strategies to appeal to these younger investors.[2] And what do these younger generations want? Technology. Millennial investors are seeking advisors who can use technology to enhance their services, and one-third of them are willing to switch advisors to meet that requirement.[3]

In the last two years we've seen this demand for technology impact the financial services industry. In 2015, Fidelity's $250 million purchase of eMoney caused quite a stir. The firm immediately rolled out its next generation emX platform and integrated with more than two dozen applications, from MoneyGuidePro and Morningstar to Redtail and Albridge.

Another significant industry change occurred in 2016 with the Department of Labor's Fiduciary Rule, resulting in much more stringent rules and regulations for recommending products and services to clients. And this is just the tip of the iceberg. Bill Morrissey, an Investment News writer, summed it up in a recent article:

> *"Financial advisers today face more uncertainty and potential headwinds than ever before — the Department of Labor's pending fiduciary ruling, rising technology and compliance costs, and increased regulatory scrutiny are just a few of the significant concerns. As a result of these and other issues, the broker-dealer industry is at a crossroads and is consolidating at an accelerated pace, unlike any period I have seen in my 30-plus years in the industry."[4]*

HOW THESE CHANGES AFFECT YOUR MARKETING

These changes to the financial services industry make inbound marketing more important than ever. The only way you can remain relevant in a competitive industry, gain trust, and stand out from the crowd is through compelling and creative marketing efforts. I've seen more advisors embrace digital marketing in the past two years than I saw in the last decade, so it's clear that you, as a member of this tech-savvy population, already understand the new way to peel the banana.

In this second edition we will increase your marketing effectiveness by helping you embrace the newest inbound marketing strategies, brand your business, and create relevant, educational, and inspiring content that you can distribute through multiple digital channels.

AN OLD MESSAGE WITH A NEW LOOK

When I think about content and digital marketing, I can't help but think about my two daughters, Andrea and Alison. While it's impossible not to be biased, I believe that they are two of the best digital marketers out there, and they don't work for an advertising agency or within a marketing department. They, like you, are small business owners.

Andrea runs Tubby Todd Bath Co., which provides 100% natural bath products for kids, and Alison runs *The Alison Show*, an all-too-appropriately-named blog that offers online courses on event hosting. In the process of building successful businesses, they've become savvy digital marketers, and as a result, I've seen both of their online sales explode. They report that they see the greatest increase in sales and web traffic when they post new content, whether it's a blog, a tweet, or an Instagram post.

Does the world need another bath product or party idea? Technically, no. There are millions of craft ideas and soap available on the market already. So why have their businesses succeeded when many others haven't? Their marketing efforts are centered on building a community and connecting with followers. It's a lesson that should not be lost on advisors, whose main objective is to build relationships of trust with clients.

Your message as an advisor can be stated in just a few words: Trust me to handle your finances. Whatever degree of service you offer, you are basically reaching out to people and asking them to trust you with their money. Building a relationship of trust with clients and prospects is something that the Internet, with its large reach yet very personal delivery systems, is uniquely suited to accomplish. Your message may be an old one, but some of the methods to deliver it are quite new and require a new skill set.

Most advisors are well aware that they need to be actively involved in digital marketing, but each day holds only so many hours, and marketing can get easily pushed to the side. The answer to the other big question — "How do I do this and still focus my time on my clients and business?" — will be explained in more detail throughout this book. I will show you ways to work smart to become an effective marketer in the digital age. In creating this new and updated version of *The Art of Inbound Marketing*, my goal is to help you do three things:

1. GET OUT OF THE BLEACHERS AND HIT THE FIELD

A few years ago, many advisors weren't on the inbound marketing train yet. I spoke with many advisors who couldn't imagine giving up their paper handouts to join social media. Now, advisors have begun to see the power of inbound marketing. If you've spent any time reading *Financial Planning* or *The Wall Street Journal*, you know technology and digital marketing are here to stay, because they work. They make life simpler, save you time, and help you do more for less money.

A couple of years ago, my wife, Marilyn, and I purchased a Georgian Manor Playhouse from Costco for our grandkids. In the store, the playhouse looked amazing. However, when we received the delivery, it was a couple of big, flat boxes with about 200-odd pieces inside. It was a good thing my grandchildren couldn't hear what I was muttering under my breath during the 20 hours it took to put the playhouse together!

The playhouse is similar to marketing. It's intimidating to look at a pile of pieces and assemble something blindly. But with instructions, perseverance, and a little sweat, you can build just about anything. With the right instructions, you can assemble a strong foundation for inbound marketing success just as you would the playhouse. Once you've completed this book and you have a stronger understanding of the pieces of marketing and how they fit together, you'll feel much more confident and ready to start marketing or improve on what you're already doing.

2. UNDERSTAND THE LATEST TRENDS AND CHOOSE WHAT WILL WORK FOR YOU

The constant evolution of marketing is a double-edged sword. On the upside, experts are refining strategies and helping you market better, stronger, and faster for less time and money. On the downside, it can be hard to keep up with the latest trends. For a financial advisor who is, first and foremost, a business professional and not a marketer, your focus is on finding the sweet spot between these two roles to accomplish your objectives.

In this book, I share how marketing has changed in the last few years, but focus on the strategies and trends that have proven their place in the industry. Don't let new platforms, trends, or jargon intimidate you. Just because marketing changes rapidly doesn't mean you have to throw your current strategies out the window. I want to show you how you can make small tweaks and adjustments to stay up to date with today's marketing successes.

3. HOW TO USE CONTENT AS THE CORNERSTONE OF YOUR MARKETING EFFORTS

If there's one facet of marketing that has exploded in the last few years, it's content. I'll go so far as to say that without continual, fresh content — whether it's originally written or shared from another source — your marketing will struggle. With around 250,000 financial advisors in the U.S.[5] and growing robo-advisor platforms that are expected to reach $489 billion in assets under management by 2020,[6] compelling content is what will differentiate you from other advisors and help you stay relevant in the industry.

One of the best things about content is this: you don't have to create it yourself. You can curate content, use evergreen content, recycle original content, and distribute content on multiple channels. You can potentially use one piece of content for months through different formats and on various channels. In this book, you'll learn how to create and find content that fits your brand and messaging and distribute it through both automated and manual efforts.

WHAT THIS BOOK IS NOT

This book is intended to complement the information you receive from your broker-dealer about digital marketing. Though we will teach you basic digital marketing principles, every firm has different guidelines for compliance. Your home office should guide you with that. Always check with your home office before executing any digital marketing campaign to learn the specific rules and regulations of your broker-dealer. Each broker-dealer has different requirements, compliance policies, and archiving protocols for communication with the public.

This book is also not a set-in-stone marketing rulebook. While I've been helping financial advisors market their businesses for decades, I think marketing is a little like the markets; no one can predict what will happen in the future. Marketing is always changing, and the results will be different for everyone. There are too many variables to say with 100% certainty that a strategy will work. I encourage you to use this book as a guideline and take creative liberties when planning and executing your marketing.

Before we jump into specific marketing vehicles and platforms, let's further explore the evolution of marketing, how content became the king of marketing, and the pieces that make up a comprehensive inbound marketing plan.

CHAPTER 1:

DRIVING THE DRIFTED AUDIENCE BACK TO YOU

Over the last two decades, the way people consume content has shifted dramatically. Twenty years ago, for example, if you created a two-hour seminar with direct mail pieces and a workbook, you could get a predictable response on that piece, gather a crowd of 20 to 30, and present your message. Those were the days when consumers read the ads in the paper and watched the commercials on TV. If they wanted to do research on a particular product, the information available was relatively limited. The marketers held most of the cards and consumers were at their mercy.

But soon, cable news was followed by cable TV, and then the VHS player offered the freedom to record a show for later. Since then, the audience that was once captive in front of the TV from dinnertime to bedtime has drifted away from marketers. New technologies have paved the way for information to be disseminated faster than ever before. Consumers have discovered that there are much more convenient ways to assimilate content on their own timetable.

TALK THE TALK

AUDIENCE DRIFT:
The movement away from traditional marketing channels (such as television, radio, and newspapers) toward digital and social media channels.

This movement places content consumption in the control of the consumer.

"Audience drift" is a term that refers to how the control of content consumption has moved into the hands of the consumer. Whether consumers are shopping, researching a purchase, or educating themselves, they are now in control of when and how they get information.

Your audience is consuming information online. The Internet has surpassed all other avenues for marketing, shopping and education—particularly for high-net-worth individuals. Add the rise of social media, which has given the consumer another unique way to consume content, and you will see that the playing field has completely changed.

THOSE IN HIGHER-INCOME HOUSEHOLDS ARE MORE LIKELY TO USE THE INTERNET

Among all American adults, the % who use the internet, by income

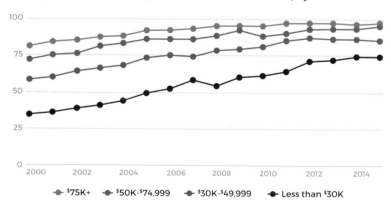

Source: Pew Research Center surveys, 2000-2015.

DO YOU GET IT AND ARE YOU ON BOARD?

At FMG Suite, I like to call our team members "smart creatives." They're intelligent individuals with unique creative capabilities, whether they're designers, marketers, or project managers. When we hire smart creatives, I like to ask them two questions:

1. **DO YOU GET IT?**
2. **ARE YOU ON BOARD?**

These two questions resonate throughout our office and are printed on our walls. It's not enough to "get" marketing and understand its relevance. You also have to be on board and completely invested in the process.

In the last few years, advisors have experienced firsthand the impact of audience drift. It's harder to get people to attend your community events, read an article, or comment on your social media posts. As the Internet gets more and more crowded with content, consumers expect immediate gratification and have a short attention span. Advisors get this. They know the audience has drifted, but they don't know how to get them back in the boat and carefully moor it to shore. Now that you get it, it's time to decide if you're on board. Are you ready to adjust your strategies to see better results?

THE POWER OF EACH: EDUCATING AND CONNECTING HONESTLY

Before I was a marketer, I was a financial planner. But even when I was a financial planner, I had a marketing mentality. I knew early on, long before content marketing was popular, that education should be at the heart of a financial advisor's marketing strategies. Education has the power to instill confidence, trust, and loyalty. It helps your clients feel more at ease with their strategies and more confident in your abilities.

In both my own experiences and through research, it became clear to me that the more fully informed someone can be, the better decisions they can make, and the more inclined they'll be to work with the advisor who provided the information. When I shifted from financial planner to marketer, I focused on creating seminars and presentations that would educate clients and motivate them to take action. Eventually the company I founded became the largest provider of marketing materials to the industry, and all of our products were based on the goal to inform and educate the consumer, then inspire them to action.

Content that educates and connects with consumers honestly is even more important since the rise of online blogs and, more recently, the Department of Labor's Fiduciary Rule. As blogs have gained traction, consumers have lost trust in the mass media. There's too much noise on television, in the newspapers, and on the radio.

AMERICAN'S TRUST IN THE MASS MEDIA

In general, how much trust and confidence do you have in the mass media—such as TV and radio—when it comes to reporting the news fully, accurately, and fairly—a great deal, a fair amount, not very much at all?

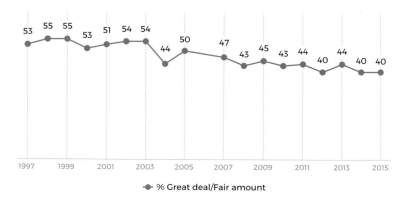

Source: Gallup trend since 1997

Consumers are now turning to the Internet for advice. Compared to the 40% of consumers who trust the mass media, more than 80% trust information and advice from blogs and 61% have made a purchase based on a blog post.[7] Why have online materials gained so much traction as the mass media falters? It comes down to education versus manipulation. The average American views advertisements and, to a certain extent, the mass media as manipulative and biased. Content created or shared by an individual or small business that educates is much more trustworthy. Marketers know this, which is why inbound marketing and content marketing have become interchangeable in these last few years.

TALK THE TALK

BLOG:
A regularly updated website or web page that features informational material, such as articles, videos, infographics, images, and presentations. The term "blog" was originally coined in 1997 when John Barger called his site a "weblog."

The Department of Labor's new Fiduciary Rule reflects what research has already revealed are investors' greatest needs in an advisor. Affluent investors want an advisor with a fiduciary responsibility so they can feel more confident knowing their advisor is serving their best interests. Advertising and blatant sales materials don't inspire much confidence. Educational content does. An advisor's value now lies in education, and the best way to do this is through content.

NO TRUST, NO NEED, NO HELP, NO HURRY

While the primary goal of content marketing is to educate rather than sell, a good content strategy should help a consumer overcome four hurdles:

1. **NO TRUST**
2. **NO NEED**
3. **NO HELP**
4. **NO HURRY**

These are the top four reasons why people don't purchase a product from a company or enlist you as their advisor. Through inbound marketing, your goal is to resolve these four concerns. Let's dive into each one a little deeper.

NO TRUST

While only 6% of Internet users have fallen prey to an online scam, 86% are concerned about becoming a victim.[8] This instills an immediate mistrust of shoddy websites. The website is the new storefront, and 70% of people surveyed claimed that they would not work with a business if their website was poorly designed or outdated.[9] Providing regular content and maintaining an up-to-date website helps you build trust with prospects.

A lack of trust also occurs in reaction to a lack of communication. Studies show that the strongest client–advisor relationships form when an advisor connects with his or her clients 12 to 18 times a year. Through content, email newsletters, and social media posts, you can connect with your clients on a regular basis and maintain a strong line of communication.

NO NEED

You don't know what you don't know. Though the average consumer knows they have to plan decades ahead for retirement, that they can mitigate taxes, or that there are ways to build their wealth faster and better than leaving it in a savings account, they may not see how urgent the need is to take action in these areas. As a consumer receives information on a regular basis regarding the importance of retirement planning or the debt management mistakes people make, they discover that they do need help from an advisor. Content and inbound marketing is about feeding information to prospects, referrals, and cold leads who may not be ready to work with you — yet — but really do need your services. Digital content marketing helps show them that need.

NO HELP

A prospect needs to know that you are the individual that can help them improve their financial situation and answer their questions. If they aren't confident in your ability or if they don't see your desire to help, they'll either keep managing their own money or find another advisor. Advertising and blatant sales tactics *tell* prospects you are knowledgeable and can help. Content and inbound marketing *shows* them that you are committed to educating them, have the knowledge and ability to help, and are uniquely qualified to address their specific concerns in an objective manner.

NO HURRY

If a prospect doesn't understand the gravity of financial planning or the importance of your services, they aren't going to contact you immediately. This can happen even if they trust you, understand the need, and believe you can help them. Through your content and marketing, you must create a sense of urgency to inspire action. How does procrastination impact compound interest? What happens if you wait another five years before you start planning for retirement? While you don't want to use scare tactics or push someone into doing anything, you can't expect a prospect to adhere to your ideal timeline if you don't set a path for them to follow.

PRO TIP:
*"My research shows **71% of households** with $1 million in investable assets are actively looking for sources of new information to help them invest. It's not a great leap to go from looking for sources of new information to looking for a new advisor."* - Richard Weylman, founder of The Weylman Center for Excellence in Practice Management[10]

WHAT DOES THIS MEAN FOR YOU?

Advisors must overcome the communication gap to reach out successfully to new prospects and referrals. Today's investors expect trustworthy education and honest communication from their advisor. If they don't feel these needs are being met, they'll look elsewhere. And they have become savvy judges of your digital outreach, so it needs to be top-notch.

As marketing evolves, so must your marketing strategies. Content is now at the center of a dynamic inbound marketing strategy and is key for driving that drifted audience back to you. In the next couple of chapters, we'll look closer at the elements that make up a strong marketing strategy and review a step-by-step guide for assembling a marketing campaign.

At FMG Suite, we've worked with thousands of financial advisors, and many of them describe themselves as educators. I don't think the average consumer understands how large a role education plays in an advisor–client relationship. That's what makes relevant, informative, and engaging content so important for advisors, and it's how you overcome those four hurdles we discussed earlier.

The best way to understand the power of content is by example. As you read articles in the *Wall Street Journal* or scan shared posts on your LinkedIn feed, make a note of which ones catch your attention. Why did you read them? What caught your eye? Was the message compelling? Did you feel inspired to take action after reading it?

Next, look at the most popular articles online. These are the homepage stories on news sites and the articles with the most likes and shares on social media. Try to identify why these stories are hits and others aren't. Why are consumers (including your target markets) drawn to these pieces? What problems do they solve? How do they encourage readers to take action?

While you don't want to plagiarize, use those popular stories as inspiration when you create your content, whether it's following a similar format or writing on the same topic. Add your own spin on it and don't forget to let your personality shine through. You'll come across as much more authentic and relatable.

As you produce, curate, and share content, keep track of the progress and results, whether you use sophisticated software or use a simple spreadsheet. What pieces are hits? Which ones missed the mark? Do more of what works and less of what didn't. It's the best way to progress and improve every month.

When done with integrity, outbound marketing has an important job in the inbound world.

CHAPTER 2:

THE ROLE OF OUTBOUND MARKETING IN YOUR INBOUND STRATEGY

If you're scratching your head after reading the title of this chapter, you're not alone. That's how my marketing team at FMG Suite felt when I told them I've changed my opinion on outbound marketing. "But wait," they said, "isn't this book titled *The Art of Inbound Marketing*?"

They weren't wrong. I'm still promoting inbound marketing as the key to success. But in the last few years, I have begun to see that outbound marketing can still play an effective role in your overall strategy. It all started when we were involved in a collaboration with one of the largest broker-dealers in the industry. Their CMO is one of the most highly regarded Chief Marketing Officers in the financial services industry. I've always admired her creativity and understanding of the role marketing plays in a financial advisor's business.

We spoke years ago, around the time I was writing the first edition of this book, and she told me, "Craig, I get what you're saying about inbound marketing and I agree. But I still believe

TALK THE TALK

OUTBOUND MARKETING:
The more traditional forms of marketing, including advertising on radio, TV, in newspapers, cold calling, and direct paper mail.

INBOUND MARKETING:
Marketing that earns the attention of customers, makes the company easy to find and draws customers in by disseminating engaging and educational content, usually in a digital format. Inbound marketing tools include blogs, interactive websites, email, and social media platforms.

CONTEMPORARY OUTBOUND MARKETING:
A marketing strategy that combines both inbound and outbound principles. While the foremost goal of inbound marketing is to educate in a non-sales manner, and outbound marketing's goal is to generate sales, contemporary outbound marketing strikes a balance between the two. Examples include sending birthday e-cards, sharing third-party content on social media, and writing a blog on how your services can benefit people.

that outbound marketing has a place in today's content-rich world." We agreed to disagree until I started looking at outbound marketing through a contemporary lens and reconsidered my position.

Now, there are a few caveats here. First, we know that the age-old ways of outbound marketing, such as billboards, mailers, and brochures, aren't as effective as they used to be. Consumers are flocking away from the manipulative advertising of the 1990s and turning to the Internet. When I talk about outbound marketing today I'm not talking about these antiquated methods, which is why I've coined a new term: *contemporary* outbound marketing.

The second caveat is that contemporary outbound marketing must be done with integrity. Different studies have shown that we are exposed to thousands of advertisements every day. And because U.S. adults are spending, on average, 10 hours and 39 minutes a day consuming media, it is critical for financial advisors to ensure their message stands out.[11] One way to do this is by coalescing inbound marketing and contemporary outbound marketing.

THE MAGNET VERSUS THE MEGAPHONE

In the previous edition of *The Art of Inbound Marketing*, we talked about the difference between being a magnet versus a megaphone. Outbound marketing (or traditional advertising) seeks to reach as many people as possible with one blanket message. You're essentially standing at a street corner and blasting your message through a megaphone. Thousands of people may see or hear your message, but few will respond. But there are certain times when that blast through the megaphone can strengthen your efforts.

Let's look at how contemporary outbound marketing can play a role in your inbound marketing strategy. In June of 2016, we saw a significant change when the United Kingdom voted to leave the European Union. The markets plummeted, investors made rash moves, clients frantically called their advisors, and no one knew what the outcome would be, both in the short-term and long-term. It's times like these when outbound marketing methods can help remind clients of the importance of a competent advisor.

One advisor sent out this email to her contacts the morning after the Brexit vote:

We woke up on Friday morning, June 24, to headlines about another economic crisis coming out of Europe. This time, the "crisis" is the decision by the U.K. to leave the European Union (EU). A somewhat unexpected outcome of a much-talked-about event, it has rocked markets around the world, including here in the U.S. In the immediate aftermath of the vote, futures were down significantly, showing that the concern is real. You may well share that concern.

Should we be worried? No more than usual. As markets start to process the likely length of the exit process, and as more clarity comes from both the EU and the U.K. around likely outcomes, markets will gradually settle down into a new normal again, as they have done historically.

Your portfolio was built with the expectation that markets would occasionally face this kind of event, so it is structured to ride it out without putting your long-term goals at risk.

We will, of course, continue to monitor the situation, but we believe that volatility in the near term is probably not worth reacting to.

This is an excellent example of inbound marketing. This advisor sent out an email to her clients and prospects without any call to action. She only wanted to educate them on what the current events mean for their finances. Of course, if they wanted more guidance they could reach out, but her only motivation was to assure her clients that they were taken care of.

With a few small tweaks, we can make this email reflect a contemporary outbound marketing strategy. Rather than providing all the answers within the email, state the facts, lead into some questions investors may have (or should have) and then offer to schedule an appointment to discuss more details on how this vote may affect an investor's portfolio. You're still providing education and drawing your readers in, but you're also advertising your expertise and services in the hopes of gaining business. Let's see how that might work:

We woke up on Friday morning, June 24, to headlines about another economic crisis coming out of Europe. This time, the "crisis" is the decision by the U.K. to leave the European Union (EU). A somewhat unexpected outcome of a much-talked-about event, it has rocked markets around the world, including here in the U.S. In the immediate aftermath of the vote, futures were down significantly, showing that the concern is real. You may well share that concern.

Should you be worried? If your portfolio were built with the expectation that markets would occasionally face this kind of event, it would ride this out without putting your long-term goals at risk. At ABC Financial Services, we create financial portfolios that help you pursue your long-term objectives and ride out the inevitable storms of the marketplace.

If you have loved ones or friends who aren't feeling confident with their portfolios, refer them to us. We'd be happy to review their current investments and whether or not adjustments may be appropriate.

Another example of contemporary outbound marketing involves decisions about content curation and sharing on social media. You likely follow companies that share plenty of posts that don't affect their "bottom line." (If every post a company shared was about their products and crafted to make sales, you would probably unfollow them!) The best social media pages feature a combination of outbound messaging, such as announcing a new service or portfolio review opportunity, and inbound, whether it's sharing an article from a newspaper or a photo from a recent firm event.

This all drives back to the common thread of both inbound and contemporary outbound marketing: integrity. Whether you're sending out an event invitation through the mail, sharing a Forbes article on Twitter, or writing a blog post, everything you produce and release into the Internet ether must be done with integrity and must educate, not manipulate.

TEN MINUTES TODAY

Scan through your past few months of email newsletters, social media posts, and website content you've produced or shared and classify it as inbound, outbound, or contemporary outbound marketing. You'll likely see that there's a fine line between inbound and contemporary outbound, which basically just adds a direct invitation onto some educational material. See which marketing methods you use the most, and how you could adjust the messaging, such as turning an outbound strategy into an inbound, or vice versa.

THREE MAIN TYPES OF CONTENT

Let's look at the three types of content that should make up your content marketing strategy, whether you're using inbound or outbound methods.

EVERGREEN

Evergreen content is content that is more general, informative, and educational. An evergreen article may be something along the lines of, "10 Tips for Managing Debt," or "A Guide to Life Insurance." It never really expires, therefore, staying "fresh" longer. Evergreen content makes it easier to stay connected with your prospects and clients on a regular basis, whether it's on social media, through email, or on your website.

Producing customized, specific content multiple times a week can be draining. I would go so far as to say that 95% of advisors don't have the time, resources, or department to create unique content every day or every few days, nor do they need to. Creating original content and implementing a content marketing strategy becomes much less intimidating when you have evergreen content to sprinkle in between your original and curated posts.

At FMG Suite, we create hundreds of evergreen pieces, including videos, articles, and presentations. This allows advisors to push out content to their audience on a regular basis without having to do the work themselves.

CURATED

Curated content includes articles, videos, infographics, presentations, and other pieces created by other sources that you share on your social media or through email. Unlike evergreen content, curated content typically focuses on timely topics and current events. This type of content helps you stay in frequent communication with your contacts and show that you are up to date on market trends and news. Some examples of curated content include articles from your favorite publications (but not direct competitors) that you link to or share. This could be an article on Social Security from the *Wall Street Journal*, or a retirement study released by your broker-dealer.

Curated content is a great way for advisors to dive deeper into topics that interest their clients, research any industry changes, and assure clients that you understand their biggest interests. And because curated content is written from many different perspectives, consumers can experience the same topic shared in a variety of ways.

PERSONAL

Personal content is the most challenging and time-consuming to create but is an essential component of your content marketing. Personal content transforms your website and social media platforms from an online brochure to high-touch, personal outreach. Some examples of personal content could be pictures from a recent charity event that your business participated in, a big life event like the birth of a grandchild, photos from a recent family vacation, or an article on how you got into the business or your investment philosophy.

These three forms of content, when used wisely, can help inform, educate, and motivate your clients. They can also help generate leads and new business. While generating business may be your bottom line as a financial advisor, taking an active role in your content marketing may also help establish yourself as a thought leader in your industry.

THOUGHT LEADERSHIP AND MARKETING

What do leaders like Steve Jobs, Seth Godin, and Thomas Edison have in common? Although they created legacies in very different industries, they were all considered thought leaders. So what exactly is thought leadership? And what does it mean for your practice?

Thought leaders are "the informed opinion leaders and the go-to people in their field of expertise."[12] They work to move or inspire others with innovative ideas and usually have a dedicated following that helps them replicate and scale their ideas and create change in their industry.

While there is no exact roadmap to becoming a thought leader, most have attained that distinction through savvy digital communication. Using the same techniques, you can join this group of elite innovators, and become a source of information and inspiration to your clients.

> **PRO TIP:**
> *"Thought leadership should be an entry point to a relationship. Thought leadership should intrigue, challenge, and inspire even people already familiar with a company. It should help start a relationship where none exists, and it should enhance existing relationships."* – Daniel Rasmus, marketing strategist and industry analyst

WHO CAN BE A THOUGHT LEADER?

There are no rules on what a thought leader looks like, but most thought leaders have created an exceptional product, service, or company. This is a good stepping stone because followers are more likely to trust someone who has something great to share. This product could be as simple as offering a unique service model, or as drastic as creating a revolutionary smartphone. Identify what is unique about the services you offer, or the way you offer them, and you will find the key to your thought leadership effort. The trick isn't to fit a criterion but instead make the decision to dedicate time, energy, and resources into a robust content marketing strategy that emphasizes your strengths. Strong content is the gateway to becoming a thought leader online.

WHY SHOULD I BECOME A THOUGHT LEADER?

In the marketing world, there is a term called "strategic visibility." Strategic visibility is getting in front of people who matter and will take action. By being a thought leader, you become a go-to resource of information for your clients and prospects while increasing your strategic visibility. You'll expose your ideas and innovations to the right amount, and the right type, of people.

Another benefit of being a thought leader is that it aids in building your credibility. Imagine two service professionals: one has an outdated website, never shares anything on social media, and only communicates with his core group of clients. The second has a beautiful, informative website full of helpful content, posts strong content on social media regularly, and takes the time to communicate with his various audiences. Which professional would you be more likely to trust, or refer to a friend? The second professional is an example of a thought leader.

WHERE THOUGHT LEADERSHIP AND CONTENT MARKETING MEET

Becoming a thought leader isn't an overnight process. Just as creating an effective content marketing strategy takes time and dedication, becoming a thought leader in your industry is no different. Inbound marketing is the first step on this long and fulfilling journey.

Content is king. You are competing with every other professional publishing content in your industry, meaning that your content needs to be unique, fresh, and informative. The better the content, the more it gets shared; and the more it gets shared, the more your strategic visibility will increase.

Another thing to consider when deciding on your content is to examine what questions your audience has and how you can help answer them. Education and guidance are excellent ways to establish yourself as a beacon of clarity and insight in a sea of content. Be an educator, not a salesperson.

Once you've first established your inbound marketing content, you can incorporate outbound methods to create your contemporary outbound marketing strategy. While your top focus should be education, you can still market your firm and services in a sophisticated manner that doesn't come across as blatant advertising.

Becoming an innovative leader capable of change may seem overwhelming, but it is possible. Every financial advisor has the potential to educate themselves continuously, share and create compelling content, and engage with their audience by answering questions. By taking one step at a time, you can become the next thought leader in your industry.

MAKE IT HAPPEN

Once you understand the role that inbound and outbound marketing can play in your strategy, you can incorporate it into your marketing efforts. Luckily, it shouldn't be as time-consuming as creating the original content you push out.

First, open an account on a curation program, like Flipboard. Follow relevant sources of information, such as personal investing, finance, marketing, and entrepreneurship.

Some articles, such as setting up a holiday budget or saving for a summer vacation, should be shared within a specific timeframe. But some can be used to beef up your content marketing strategy down the road. Save these types of articles for later.

Think about times when you would want to reach out to your clients without the need to generate leads. In the earlier example, an advisor wanted to comfort her clients in times of market fluctuation. Brainstorm some other times when reaching out to your clients makes sense.

Having a thought out, carefully crafted content strategy will set your firm apart.

CHAPTER 3:

PREPARING YOUR CONTENT STRATEGY RECIPE

It's Saturday night and you are settling down to binge-watch a series on Netflix. You get very hungry for your favorite chocolate chip cookies, just like the ones Mom used to make. You know the recipe; you've made them dozens of times, so you run to the kitchen and quickly mix up a batch. You patiently wait the required amount of time, pull the cookies out of the oven, and...they're flat. You quickly run through the recipe in your head and realize — drat! — you forgot to add the baking soda. There is nothing you can do about it now, and you wish you had taken the time to get that dog-eared cookbook out of the cupboard and follow the recipe.

Smart bakers know the importance of adding all the ingredients in a recipe. And smart marketers understand the necessity of including all the crucial elements of a content marketing strategy. As you work toward becoming a master chef, you'll discover how to add the right ingredients to set your efforts apart from the competition.

PRO TIP:

NewsCred Head of Strategy, Michael Brenner, is a content expert. He suggests that in order to create content that your clients will love, you need to talk to them, ask questions, and then leverage the information your firm already has. *"50% of the content you need is already present in your information."* Audit your existing content, understand your client's needs, and adjust ingredients as needed.[13]

5 STEPS TO BUILDING YOUR CONTENT STRATEGY

An effective inbound marketing plan consists of a carefully coordinated combination of digital outreach activities, including email, website design, presentations, blogs, and social media posts. Here are five steps that will act as a recipe for success when building your content strategy.

STEP 1: HAVE A DOCUMENTED STRATEGY

Documentation is essential. It keeps you and your staff on the same page and helps you stay consistent, on track, and on schedule with your content marketing. Before you start baking a cake, you need a written recipe. The same is for your content strategy. Document the key elements of your strategy, including needs, budget, timing, and resources you'll need.

STEP 2: GROW YOUR NETWORK

Your network is your marketing base. Build your list of contacts one name at a time, starting with all of the contacts you have now. Confirm you have all the correct contact information and send out a welcome email previewing the great marketing content you have coming. When you meet someone new, get in the habit of asking for their email or business card. Once you've been working with a client for six months or a year, talk with them about any friends or family they think would like being on your email list.

Don't wait to meet someone in person to exchange information. LinkedIn is one of the best places (both on- and offline) to network with potential clients and strategic partners. Spend just 15 minutes per day on LinkedIn and you'll quickly grow your network and connect with people you may otherwise have never met in person. We'll talk about LinkedIn later on in the book, so stay tuned for a more in-depth discussion on how to use this social media platform to your advantage.

STEP 3: MAP YOUR CLIENT JOURNEY

Also known as the customer journey, this refers to a diagram or map that illustrates the steps your clients take in engaging with your firm on their route to becoming a client. There's no right number of touchpoints an advisor will have, as it depends on your intended market, your content, and how you conduct business. But you should have a clear sense of the steps your clients take, from first contact to a working relationship. Then you can create content to make this journey easier for both you and your potential clients.

Mapping out the client journey helps ensure that you address everything a prospect would want to know about you and your services before doing business with you. Most questions that clients have will be at the early stages of the journey, so you should dedicate a significant amount of content to addressing these early questions. These may be as simple as, "what does a financial advisor do?" or "why do I need to work with an advisor?" Tackle these basic questions first before diving into more complex investment strategies.

STEP 4: MATCH YOUR CONTENT TO YOUR
TARGET MARKET

Now that you have a network, you need content to share with them. Your content should be directed to a few distinct target markets (and no, it doesn't count to say that your target market is anyone with money to invest!). Choose two or three niche markets and build an inbound marketing strategy that addresses each one.

For example, if you are targeting small business owners, you might run a series of video vignettes about estate preservation or pension plan options. Supplement this financial information with fun surveys for business owners to take or articles on relevant topics, from entrepreneurship to the best company meeting ideas. Or, if you are targeting women investors, publish timely articles on your LinkedIn about the unique financial concerns they may face. Or hold a monthly dinner for women only, to get your female clients more involved in financial planning. There are many options, but the point is to have your content strategy grow organically from your target market.

In the next chapter, we'll go over content with a fine-toothed comb and share how to determine the types of content to create, curate, distribute, and recycle.

STEP 5: PLAY TO YOUR STRENGTHS; HIRE OUT YOUR WEAKNESSES

You likely entered the financial services industry because you enjoy finance and the opportunity to help people. My guess is that you're not a trained web designer or marketing expert, nor should you be (as they say, a Jack of all trades is a master of none). You want to focus your time and energy on providing financial services to your clients. While you can certainly maintain your marketing strategies, it's best to rely on experts for larger projects, including web design, video production, graphic design, and extensive writing projects.

When it comes to marketing, I like to set boundaries for myself. Unless it's a project I'm particularly passionate about, I rely on help if a marketing task is going to take me more than two hours to complete. Spending 10 or 12 hours creating a video may be interesting, but may not be the most productive use of your time. If you use FMG Suite, you're familiar with the high quality of videos and content we create. As much as I'd like to take credit for it, I don't create those videos or each individual website. I rely on a team of experts that specialize in different fields, be it writing, design, or video production. You should do the same.

It's wise to have a professional designer take the lead with your website, have a video company create your videos, and work with a professional writer for lengthier projects (or hire a company like ours that combines all three services). In order to be consistent, you need to delegate the parts of inbound marketing that you don't like doing and leave yourself time and energy to do what you do best.

THE EVOLUTION OF MARKETING

When this book was first published, these three steps of building a content strategy were sufficient for advisors getting started with inbound marketing. But today, in a world where everyone is creating and sharing content, you have to go a step further. *Entrepreneur* explains it best when it says:

> *"Effective marketing is often what separates rapidly growing companies from slow-growing or stalled companies that started at the same time, serve the same market and offer similar merchandise."*[14]

Let's look at one way to do just that.

BY THE NUMBERS
Over 75% of email revenue is generated by triggered campaigns, rather than one-size-fits-all campaigns.[15] And **53% of marketers** say ongoing, personalized communication with existing customers results in moderate to significant revenue impact.[16]

MARKETING CAMPAIGNS

The word "campaign" is one of those terms that may sound vaguely familiar, but it's hard to articulate an exact definition or example. Your mind may jump to advertising campaigns, such as Coca-Cola's classic "I Want to Buy the World a Coke," or Apple's famous "Mac or PC" commercials. For our purposes, we are defining a campaign as a series of outreach efforts on multiple channels based on a common theme. For example, a campaign may consist of a series of emails reaching out to pre-retirees as a niche market, sending an e-card every holiday, or sharing monthly communications about the market's performance.

Campaigns generally include different ways to "touch," or contact, your clients. This may include email marketing, social media, blogging, and other marketing strategies. Successful campaigns require careful research that is well executed and focused on details, rather than rest on a single, grand idea. Campaigns range in duration, but are usually long-term projects that last anywhere from a few months to over a year.

CREATING YOUR CAMPAIGN

Every campaign is different, and therefore they will involve different strategies. However, there are a few common threads that tie together some of the best campaigns.

1. **Address a target market**
   Do some research about where your clients are and what they're thinking about. A good marketing campaign will provide the solution to some of their most pressing concerns.

2. **Emphasize your mission statement or unique value proposition**
   Ask yourself who you serve, what you have to offer, and why people should work with you instead of the competition.

3. **Employ a variety of different platforms**
   Some marketing strategies include seminars, advertising, blogging, email newsletters, social media, print media, cold calling, and referrals. Your marketing techniques will depend on what you want your clients and prospects to do after viewing your campaign.

4. **Monitor your campaigns and make changes as necessary.**

   Just as your website or social media profiles should be dynamic and ever-changing, so should your marketing campaign. Analyze your data, regularly view your analytics, and make changes to your outreach efforts.

These are just some of the building blocks of a campaign. From here, you can start to build out your own unique strategy and find out what works best for your firm. In today's media world, there is so much noise that one outreach effort may not be enough to make a difference. Campaigns are a great way to continue to touch your clients and prospects with ongoing communication based on what they care about.

TEN MINUTES TODAY

In order to fully understand campaigns, it's helpful to see some in action. Spend some time researching marketing campaigns. What makes them successful? Can you use some of these practices in your future campaigns?

MAKE IT HAPPEN

As you can tell, marketing campaigns take a great deal of patience, dedication, and research. That said, though, the effort will be worth it because clients will be able to see the hard work you put into your marketing strategy. The series of touches will show that you care, the common theme will be directly tailored to what they want to hear, and you will set yourself apart from other marketers in your field. So what are we waiting for? Let's get started!

1. **Quantify your goals**

   Different campaigns have different goals, including generating more leads, nurturing current clients, celebrating, and many more. Figure out what you want to accomplish with your campaign and develop it accordingly.

2. **Think of your target audience**

   Where are they? What are their biggest concerns? How often are they on social media or email? Questions like these will also help you segment your lists and send specialized campaigns to different markets.

3. **Generate campaign ideas and strategies**

   This may be the most difficult part, but is the meat of your strategy. Outline enough emails, social media posts, and other marketing mediums that will cover at least six months. For example, if you are sending out a bi-monthly newsletter, you will need at least 12 in your campaign arsenal.

4. **Develop a system to handle increased traffic coming from your campaign**

   With great risk comes great rewards! Make sure you are prepared for the rewards coming your way. For example, if you wrote a whitepaper to send to any clients that give you their email, make sure they get that whitepaper in a timely manner. Hiring a part-time assistant or intern to field this traffic may be a good idea.

5. **Make changes**

   Once you've developed your campaign, it may be tempting to write it down in permanent marker and never look at it again. But one of the benefits of digital marketing is that you can measure how your efforts are performing and make changes accordingly. Your campaign isn't set in stone once it starts.

If all this campaign talk has your head spinning, hiring a professional marketing team may help you streamline your process. At FMG Suite, we offer a variety of campaigns for financial advisors, including ones that educate, inform, and generate leads.

CHAPTER 4:

CREATING, USING, AND SHARING CONTENT THAT COUNTS

In today's digital marketing landscape, content is the heart of your online efforts and pumps education and information to your multiple marketing channels. Without that heartbeat, all other marketing efforts become lifeless. As I explained earlier, there's been a significant consumer shift from advertising to content. The best marketers know this, and more than 70% of marketers are creating more content now than they did in 2014.[17] Why? Because content marketing works.

On average, consumers go through 57% of the purchasing process before ever talking to someone.[18] This means your prospects and client referrals are nearly two-thirds of the way to becoming a client by the time they pick up the phone and call you or send you an email. They're first checking out your website, looking at your social media profiles, and reading your content. The better the content you provide on your channels, the more qualified and ready prospects and referrals will be when they speak with you. This cuts down on your time and efforts when nourishing a new relationship. In fact, nearly three-quarters of companies indicate that content marketing is increasing their lead quality and quantity.[19]

I have a friend named Chuck who ran a successful business for years. At the age of 62, he embarked on a second career providing online voice lessons and coaching. He had a strong business model, a modern website, and a great product. However, as months went on, he struggled to gain online followers. People weren't talking about his business, sharing his social media posts, or referring friends to his website. He shared his concern with me and, as we spoke about his business, I discovered he wasn't creating much content. I suggested he commit to creating new content on a consistent basis.

TALK THE TALK

CONTENT MARKETING:
A strategic marketing approach focused on creating, curating, and sharing content. Content should be valuable, informative, educational, and relevant. The goal is inspiring, attracting, and retaining a specific and defined ideal clientele.

A few months later, I was pleasantly surprised to see that he had done just that. Today, he has more than 100 courses on his website, and he has an enormous online following from all around the world. He continues to create content and every time he releases something new he sees a boost in his interactions. While I always believed in the power of content, this was just another example of just how much it can transform a business's online presence.

WHAT IS CONTENT?

Before we dive into content marketing, it's germane to define what "content" entails. Content refers to an extensive umbrella of types, categories, and mediums of information.

TYPES

There are three general types of content that make up a financial advisor's content marketing strategy — personal, evergreen, and curated — which I introduced in Chapter 2. These types refer to how you produce or find your content.

CATEGORIES

Just as newspapers, magazines, and blogs have categories, so does your overall content marketing strategy. These categories will define the tone and style you set for your content marketing efforts, be it casual lifestyle content, or professional and educational content. Some categories financial advisors may consider include lifestyle, educational, personal, professional, or human interest.

TOPICS

At FMG Suite, we refer to these as "matters," as they are the topics that matter the most to our clients. For an advisor, these are the topics that your ideal clientele is most interested in learning about, whether that's estate planning, investments, college planning, or debt management. We recommend sticking to a maximum of seven total matters that you cover in your content. Depending on the level of importance, you can allocate more or less energy to different matters. For instance, 70% of your content may be on business planning if your focus is on small business owners, and the other 30% on estate planning, budgeting, and other topics.

FORMAT

Content isn't limited to the written form. There are dozens of different formats and layouts for presenting your content (and this is where recycling comes into play, but more on that further in this chapter). Some of the most common formats of content include:

- Blog Post
- Video
- Image
- Presentation
- Infographic
- eBook
- Whitepaper
- Book
- Newsletter
- Quiz
- Live Stream
- Checklist
- Podcast

PRO TIP:
"The easiest way to turn off your community members is to broadcast the same message across multiple channels. Instead, determine the kind of content that interests the members of your community in a way that is useful to them." - Joe Pulizzi, founder of Content Marketing Institute[20]

THE FIVE FOUNDATIONAL NECESSITIES FOR CONTENT SUCCESS

Content marketing requires both sides of the brain. As creative as content creation is, it's also highly strategic. Before you can embark on a journey toward content success, you need a solid foundation to support your efforts. This framework entails five necessities:

1. **An easily articulated brand**

   You understand who you are, what you offer, and who your clients are. But can you describe what you do and what your practice's most important elements are in fewer than three concise sentences? A business' brand is difficult to capture, but your content and marketing efforts become a hundred times simpler and more efficient when you can eloquently define your business and what it stands for.

MORE ONLINE

Sharing how to create your brand is another topic that would require an entirely separate book! For help creating your unique branding strategy, we've created an online course, featuring a broadcast, workbook, and three labs. To get started, visit http://fmgsuite.com/branding-labs.

2. **A thorough understanding of your target market's greatest concerns and interests**

   People purchase from and work with hundreds of businesses, but they only interact with a handful on a regular basis. They follow brands on social media, read their blogs, and subscribe to their email newsletters because they relate to and enjoy the content they share. The businesses with the largest followings have a strong grasp of their client base. They know their clientele's demographics, their needs, and their interests. Much of this relates to personas, which we'll discuss later in this chapter.

3. **An organized schedule**

   The most successful marketers are organized marketers. Your content distribution must be consistent. You should be sharing your content regularly on social media, through email, and on your website. It's impossible for an advisor to balance both his or her business and marketing duties without a schedule. As you develop your content marketing strategy, determine how frequently and through which channels you can commit to posting. Start small and slowly build up your schedule. To begin, you may consider posting three times a week on social media, sending a monthly email newsletter, and adding a new piece of content to your website every month.

4. **Curation and distribution technologies**

   Online tools like Hootsuite, Sprout Social, Flipboard (and FMG Suite, of course!) cut down the amount of time you have to spend curating and distributing your content. There are hundreds of options out there, so you'll want to research to see which ones offer the features most important to you.

5. **Distribution channels**

   Creating and finding content is the first step. The second is distributing it. The distribution channels you choose will depend on your audience, but generally speaking, advisors should use a healthy mix of social media platforms, email, and their websites to share and post content.

These five elements will support all of your content marketing efforts from beginning to end.

The content you create and curate will largely depend on the first two components of your content foundation: your brand and your client base's needs. Every piece of content you create or share should align with your brand, your clients' greatest questions and needs, and the four "no" objectives we covered in Chapter 1.

This is where personas come into play. A persona is a semi-fictional depiction of your ideal client based on industry research and data about your current clients. Most big businesses today use personas and, as they gain in popularity, small businesses are following suit. While a large company may have a handful of personas, a financial advisor should stick to a maximum of three.

A persona includes client demographics, behavior patterns, motivations, and goals. The more detailed your persona, the greater insight you have into your ideal clientele. When creating a persona, you want to give them a real name and real characteristics, as it should represent a real person with whom you want to work. Think of their journey as the shift from prospect to client. What questions do they ask along the way? What language do they use in talking about your services? Where do they go to find new information? How do they share it with their friends and family? All of these questions guide the development of your personas.

At FMG Suite, we use personas to help us stay consistent in our messaging and service offerings. Before we launch a new product, create content, or send something to our clientele, we consider our relevant persona and whether or not it aligns.

By focusing on personas, you will be able to personalize your content better to speak to those you want to attract. There are any number of ways to decide how you want to segment your personas, whether you focus on assets, personality, or age. Whatever you choose, it should reflect the reality of your clientele and provide the direction you need to engage your clients with content that covers consistent topics and themes.

MORE ONLINE

Creating your personas requires time and strategy, but the work is worth the results. For more examples of personas and tips for creating them, visit FMG Suite's Resource Center to watch our broadcast, "The 5 W's of Content Marketing" and download the accompanying whitepaper, "How to Create Content that Inspires Action."

Once you've defined your personas, consider the most relevant topics and concerns on their minds so you can provide valuable insights and establish your expertise. The most compelling content offers a viable solution to a common problem. By solving a problem for your client base, you show your commitment to making their lives better. Your solutions might tie to specific products or services, or they may solely provide tips to help people achieve their desired result.

If you're having trouble with this step, consider the following five questions:

1. What is your most valuable service?
2. What topic do you never tire of discussing?
3. What knowledge do you feel you should charge for?
4. What value can you provide a person searching for a service you provide?
5. What are the big conversations to which you'd like to contribute?

You'll find that addressing these questions and overcoming the 4 "no's" go hand-in-hand. By creating and finding content that answers your ideal clientele's questions and concerns, you can build trust, identify yourself as a helpful resource, establish a need for your services, and encourage a sense of urgency.

You've built your brand and personas and have a strong grasp on how to create and find content that will connect with your ideal clientele. Now it's time to put these ideas into action.

As explained in Chapter 2 and earlier in this chapter, there are three types of content: original, evergreen, and curated. We recommend a combination of one-third original and two-thirds evergreen and curated content. Let's review how to balance these three types and keep your content cohesive.

ORIGINAL CONTENT

This is your opportunity to get personal and create highly specialized content targeting a particular client base, such as retirees, women investors, or business owners. In my experience, I've seen advisors achieve the most success with content marketing when they get personal and create original content.

When I think of successful financial advisors, some that come to mind are Deb Sims, Jeremy Stanley, Ann Zuraw, and Philip Board. All of these advisors have a target market, have branded their businesses, and create original content. Deb Sims and Ann Zuraw both go above and beyond when it comes to creating content for women, whether they're hosting financial workshops, blogging, or creating videos on social media. Jeremy Stanley has written a book specifically on financial planning for Certified Registered Nurse Anesthetists (his target market) and speaks to graduating classes. And Philip Board has combined his cycling passion with his career by blogging about marathons and participating in charitable events. All of these outreach strategies help these advisors engage with clients and prospects on a regular basis and connect with the type of people with whom they *want* to work.

As you create that original content, keep in mind the concept of forming a community. Share pictures of events happening in your clients' lives that will strike a chord with others. For example, if you have a charity that is special to you, participate in a fundraising event and feature it. Then invite other clients to share their priority projects, and post pictures of them with a description. Don't be afraid to find inspiration from other financial advisors and put your own spin on blogging, broadcasting videos, or hosting events.

EVERGREEN CONTENT

Evergreen content is important for financial advisors to utilize because it makes it easier to post consistently, share regularly, and stay relevant. While evergreen content can be the most difficult to create (as it's time-consuming and can require extensive research) there are a few ways to access evergreen content on financial topics.

At FMG Suite, this is our specialty. We've produced more than 400 videos, articles, presentations, infographics, and calculators that fall within seven categories: investing, retirement, estate, tax, insurance, lifestyle, and money. As all pieces are already FINRA-reviewed (and the statistics and data are updated every few years), you don't have to worry about gaining compliance approval. This is evergreen content that is ready to go.

If you have an easily accessible content library, (such as from FMG Suite) you can share evergreen content through social media, email, and on your website to maintain a consistent and active online presence without becoming a full-time content creator. Remember, not all evergreen content is created equal. Don't share something just for the sake of it. Only rely on content that matches your branding and meets your clientele's needs and interests.

CURATED CONTENT

If evergreen content rarely expires, curated content is the exact opposite. Timely and related to current events, curated is the content that helps financial advisors stay current and relevant. For many advisors, writing a blog post on the financial markets hours after Brexit or another major economic event can be difficult. However, to show you're still very much aware of what's going on, you can share articles that reflect your opinions and advice on the event.

Flipboard is one of my favorite apps (you'll probably hear me talk about this app several times throughout this book!) and I highly recommend it for financial advisors. Flipboard is an aggregator that collects content from social media and other websites and presents it in magazine format so you can quickly "flip" through the different articles. You can choose select categories to follow — such as business, news, and personal finance — and get news from your favorite publications on your favorite topics. Then, you can share any relevant pieces you find on social media.

CRAIG'S SECRET FOR SUCCESS

When I am judging a piece of content I've created or curated, I ask myself three simple questions:

- Does it exemplify my professional approach?
- Does it offer valuable information to the client?
- What do I want my client/prospect to do as a result of this content?

If I don't like the answer to any of those three questions, I give it a pass. This has saved me a few times! Consider these questions when creating content or sharing something produced by someone else.

CONTENT DISTRIBUTION CHANNELS

Creating and curating content is the first part of your content marketing. The next is distributing it to your audience. Some of the chapters that follow focus on the biggest channels for your content distribution. For now, let's quickly review what these are:

- Your website and blog
- Social media (Facebook, LinkedIn, and Twitter)
- Email

These are the main channels, but there are countless other places you can share your content to attract a wider (and different) audience. While these may require more time than the main three, they offer some unique opportunities to penetrate a niche market. Some of these include:

- Local newspaper
- Conference or event
- Online forum
- TV or radio show
- PR newswire

MORE ONLINE

On the FMG Suite blog, we've created a comprehensive list of lesser-known but powerful content distribution channels. If you're feeling inspired and are ready to take your content to the next level, review the list and give a few of these options a try. Check it out by visiting https://fmgsuite.com/market-in-motion/content-distribution/.

If you're looking to become a thought leader in your industry, these advanced channels can help. But for most financial advisors, these channels won't be worth the time and effort it will take to create the content and place it. Don't overwhelm yourself by trying to distribute on a dozen different channels. For now, focus on the main three: your website/blog, social media, and email.

In this digital age we live in, new content is constantly published online. While the Internet makes it easy for us to find answers to any question we have, it also makes it hard to get your piece to stand out and find an audience.

⏱ EVERY MINUTE...

🌐 571 new websites are created

🐦 Twitter users send over 100,000 tweets

𝐟 Facebook users share 684,478 pieces of content

✉ Email users send 204,166,667 messages

▶ YouTube users upload 48 hours of new video

Ⓦ Wordpress users publish 347 new blog posts

📷 Instagram users share 3,600 new photos

👍 Brands and organizations on Facebook receive 34,722 likes

Source: Mashup

With so much information shared every minute of the day, new content becomes old content very quickly.

⧗ CONTENT HAS A SHELF LIFE

🐦 Twitter Content: 2.3 hours

𝐟 Facebook Posts: 5 hours

📌 Pinterest Pins: 2 days

📰 Blog Content: 37 Days

▶ Video Content: 3 Months

Source: Skyword

You can extend the life cycle of your content by recycling and repurposing it through different channels and mediums. This not only saves you time you would have otherwise spent on creating entirely new content, but it also helps you make the most of your ideas and concepts.

My wife, Marilyn, published a book earlier this year. It was doing well, but she wanted to gain more exposure. When she told me was considering going on a book tour or speaking to local groups, I suggested a simpler option: repurposing some of the most salient points in her book in the form of blog posts that she could send to her email list on a monthly basis. She could gain more exposure as her email list grew and keep the conversation about her book going for months on end. She did so, and book sales took an upturn.

This is content recycling at its finest. You use a single idea and create multiple pieces of content about it. For example, if you had an excellent response to a Facebook post you shared about what parents need to know about education planning, you can take these essential points and turn them into a Slideshare to share on your LinkedIn.

Because the audiences of your Facebook and LinkedIn are likely going to differ, this same information will reach different dimensions of your client base. For data-focused articles, transform them into infographics or videos.

TEN MINUTES TODAY

Whenever you scan the news or your social media feed, take note of which headlines and pieces of content stand out and write down a few ideas for how you could create a similar piece that your audience would enjoy. This will make it easier to create your own unique content and you may find inspiration for topics, formats, or styles you hadn't previously considered.

A schedule is a must for recycling content consistently. Consider using a spreadsheet to manage your content schedule and recycling efforts. For example, for an article on "10 Things to Consider Before Claiming Social Security," you may transform it into a presentation, whitepaper, and infographic. In January, you'll post the article on your blog and share it on social media. In February, you'll publish it as a presentation on LinkedIn. In March, you develop it into a longer whitepaper and encourage email subscribers to download it on your website. And in April, transform it into an infographic and share it on social media and in online forums. One piece of content now has a much longer lifecycle and can hit multiple platforms several times for maximum reach.

MANAGING YOUR TIME

You can see how this kind of content creation could become a full-time job, but it doesn't need to be. If you are affiliated with a broker-dealer, you receive lots of valuable content through that channel. Additionally, there are outstanding articles, infographics, and quotes that you can share with your audience. Be careful about linking to other websites, as it requires your visitor to leave your site to view the content. Once they're gone, they're gone!

We'll talk more about different aspects of content creation in later chapters. The most important thing to remember at this point is to break out of that mode of wanting to reach people with just your name and services. Instead, concentrate on preparing nuggets of information that will impress them and keep them coming back for more. David Meerman Scott sums up the importance of meaningful content: "Smart marketers... know that the most effective web strategies anticipate needs and provide content to meet them, even before people know to ask."[21]

Rome wasn't built in a day, and neither is a content marketing strategy. But there are three simple ways you can enhance the quality of your content strategy right now.

1. Rethink your brand

Sit down with your business partner or someone who knows you and your business and talk through your brand. Who are you? How do you do business? Why are you in this business? What is your philosophy? Once you answer those questions, think about whether or not your website and your marketing reflect that. If it doesn't, it's time to change your website and marketing.

2. Collect and polish your best stories

Make a concentrated effort to pull together some compelling stories and case studies that illustrate crucial principles. Use more stories in your website copy, your presentations, and in your blogging.

3. Build community spirit by generating more conversations on your website and social sites

The goal of creating your content is to get responses and to create a conversation with your audience. Share photos from community events, host your own event, and encourage comments and shares. If someone comments on one of your posts, respond in a timely fashion.

CHAPTER 5:

KICK YOUR WEBSITE INTO HIGH GEAR

A few years ago, I was chatting with an attendant on a flight to Florida. When I told her that I was going to speak at a conference for financial advisors she suddenly grew very animated.

"What are you talking about?" she asked.

"Well, I am a digital marketing specialist, so I'll be talking about websites and..." That was as far as I got.

"Websites! Don't get me started! My husband is a financial advisor and he has this crummy old website that he has been meaning to upgrade for years, but he never gets around to it. He actually had someone tell him that they wanted to refer him to a friend but they were embarrassed to show them his website!" At this point she dug one of her husband's business cards out of her purse and gave it to me. "Since he won't listen to me, would you please call him and tell him to do something about that dated site of his?"

If only to escape to more urgent matters, I promised to do as she said. Later that week I handed the card to one of our associates and asked her to give this advisor a call. At the time, updating his website wasn't one of his top priorities, but if I had met his wife today I would like to think things would be a little different.

There are very few reasons why a small business owner shouldn't have a website in today's media age. With the advent of new technologies, you can now create a website in a matter of minutes. Creating a beautiful, user-friendly site isn't any harder than making an account, paying a monthly fee, and writing some short content.

BY THE NUMBERS

How important are the design and elements of your website? According to Adobe, **38% of people will stop engaging with a website if the content/layout is unattractive**. And in case you are wondering whether it is worth the trouble to include video, the same study shows that two-thirds of people would rather watch a video than read an article on the same topic.[22]

THE DIFFERENCE BETWEEN GOOD AND GREAT

Most financial professionals have a website. You've probably spent both time and money over the last few years to keep it up and running. But when was the last time you got a new client, or even a warm lead, from your site? If your website isn't working as hard as you are, it's time to kick it into gear. Let's look at some of the most common, and effective, design aspects that professionals recommend, and some fairly simple steps that you can take to make your website more engaging.

In the beginning of the Digital Age, financial advisors and other small business owners thought of their websites as a place to gather all the information their customers would need. They were text-heavy, full of cumbersome elements, and bogged the viewer down with overwhelming content. A website was not much more than a digital brochure.

Today, we approach websites a little differently. Rather than focusing solely on practical details, designers and marketers now focus more on branding. Your website is a chance to set the tone of your business, evoke feelings and trust in your visitors, and motivate them to reach out. While it may seem like today's websites have less content and information, they are actually doing more than the early websites; they are a snapshot into the way you do business, and the unique distinguishing characteristics of your firm.

PRO TIP:
Our Vice President of Content and Creative Services, Brandon Brown, with his extensive knowledge of website trends, notes, *"Today, designers use aspects such as minimalism, white space, and big, full-width images to provoke viewers' emotions. Fewer elements often correlate to more emotion, and more elements are often used solely for functionality."*

Think of website design as a travel experience. Having a strictly informative, straight-to-business website is like taking a group tour of a foreign country with the help of a tour guide. You are shuttled to exact points of interest, everything is explained in clear terms, and most people in the group have the same experience.

Having a website that subscribes to modern trends and leaves room for imagination is like visiting a foreign city on your own. You can eat what you want, visit the lesser-known attractions, and build your own experience. Each person's adventure is different.

While neither of these experiences is better or worse than the other, they emphasize different goals. The first is informative and straightforward, while the second is imaginative and personal.

Current design trends sway toward the second because websites are putting more emphasis on branding and user experience than ever before.

Of course, one unique consideration for financial advisors when building their sites is compliance. Compliance regulations used to be an excuse for advisors not to build a site at all, but luckily most home offices and broker-dealers are onboard with the majority of inbound marketing strategies. One major change is that since 2016, all independent financial advisors must have BrokerCheck, a background check software by FINRA, on their site. FMG Suite was proud of our timely integration of BrokerCheck into all of our advisors' websites.

TALK THE TALK

USER EXPERIENCE (ALSO KNOWN AS UX):
A term that encompasses a user's whole experience when navigating a company's site. Good UX means the site is seamless, easy to understand, and intuitive.

BACK END:
The part of a website hidden from view of regular visitors.

BELOW THE FOLD:
Information below the first visible point of a website. This information usually requires the viewer to scroll to see it.

LEGGO MY LOGO

A logo is one of the most important aspects of a website because it includes your business name and is a key part of your branding strategy. It's usually the first thing someone sees when they visit your website and, ultimately, it defines your entire business in one image. Because you'll use your logo on your website and all throughout your marketing, invest in a good one.

Go for a clean simple logo that has minimal text and no more than three different colors. Your logo file should be a high-resolution image with a transparent background.

LESS IS MORE

The best way to create a cohesive design aesthetic is to keep your website colors consistent with your logo. If you have black, burgundy, and yellow in your logo, you should find images and text that echo those colors in similar shades. Just as with the logo, it's best to stick to a maximum of three different colors throughout your website. This includes background colors, font colors, and box colors. Once you use more than three, your website can begin to look cluttered and disjointed.

Chances are, you're not a part-time web designer and all this talk is making your head spin. Luckily, there are some things you can do today to make your website more user-friendly.

PERSONALIZE AND LOCALIZE

There are approximately 300,000 independent financial advisors in the United States. The chances are that many of those advisors offer similar services and processes as your firm. But, there is only one you! So how do you convey your uniqueness to clients and prospects?

PICTURES WORTH A THOUSAND WORDS

If I had a dollar for every time I've seen a picture of hands shaking, a conference room, or a group of smiling models on an advisor's website, I would be on my own island sitting upon a pile of cash. Okay, that might be a slight exaggeration. But in all seriousness, stock photography has been done a million times over. Take a different approach with the images on your site.

Ideally, you should add real pictures of you and your team. These personal touches positively impact your website's objectives. Another benefit of personal photos is that they show visitors something they have never seen before. When potential customers visit your site for the first time, their immediate reaction should be "Wow," not "Didn't I see this picture somewhere else?"

Even if you do use stock photography, choose pictures that mean something to you. These could be your local area, the type of clients you enjoy working with, or community organizations you're involved in.

CREATIVE CONTENT

You should also personalize your website with customized content. Even if you're not a professional writer, you can still add some copy that is unique to your firm. Your bio is a great place to start.

First, lead with what matters most to your clients, which is most likely your background, education, services, and credentials.

James Mitchell is an experienced professional with over three decades in the financial services industry. He is a CFP® and a member of the National Association of Personal Financial Advisors. James Mitchell and Associates serves the community of San Diego in all areas of financial planning, including wealth management, retirement planning, estate conservation, and tax-advantaged investing.

Next, round out your bio with volunteer activities, hobbies, and family details. This helps your clients and prospects see you as relatable and someone they would want to work with.

James Mitchell graduated from UCLA, where he serves on the alumni board. He is a member of the San Diego Rotary Club and serves on the local board of Habitat for Humanity. James is active in local organizations such as the YMCA and served on the San Diego County school board from 2000–2004. He enjoys hiking and running, and has participated in several triathlons. He and his wife Jane have three children and two grandchildren. Pictures on request!

Our FMG Suite copywriters suggest using brief paragraphs and tight sentences because your reader wants the short version of your life and accomplishments. Write in the third person and remember that, while a few personal facts are interesting, too many personal details will detract from the professional tone you want to achieve. Lastly, have someone else proof your bio for typos or misspellings.

Your homepage also needs some sort of introduction to show clients and prospects who you are. Usually, the summary on a homepage isn't more than two or three paragraphs. If you're feeling too overwhelmed, try following this recipe:

1. Introduce yourself and your firm. What makes you different? Why should someone work with you?

2. Give a brief overview of your services. Remember, clients will be able to find more information deeper within your site. Just highlight some of the most important aspects.

3. Encourage them to reach out. It may be helpful to list what areas you serve or your phone number and email.

These techniques are a great place to start when personalizing and localizing your website.

SHARING IS CARING

Your visitors should have the ability to share every piece of content you post. Right next to the post, include a strong call to action, such as "Do you know someone who might be interested in this topic?"

The text should sit right above social share icons that link to Facebook, Twitter, LinkedIn, or email. Social share icons make it easy for visitors to share your content with their friends and family. If you don't invite them to share your content, they won't think to do so. If you do, though, and make it as easy as possible, chances are your clients will think of at least one person who might be interested in your video, blog, or article.

Always make sure that when the content is shared, the recipient will come back to your site. You don't want to send people to other websites instead of coming to your website and getting better acquainted with you.

A website is only as good as the leads it's able to generate. There are a few things you can do to keep visitors on your site longer, educate them while they're there, and motivate them to take further action.

FORMS

I suggest putting lead generation forms, such as "Have a Question?" on every page of your website. Every website visitor that takes the time to fill out a form is a warm lead because they are interested in your and your services. After you receive their information, follow up with a personal call within 24 hours. Using forms on every page of your website and responding quickly to them is key to converting website visitors into loyal clients.

VIDEO

Video has a profound impact on the average time a visitor spends on a website. Video slows down your website visitor, and studies show that the longer a visitor stays on the site, the more likely he or she is to become a client. Video is easy to share on social media, and gets clients wanting more information. For example, a three-minute video about retirement planning isn't enough to cover all the necessary points, but it may be enough to get your viewer motivated to call you to set up an appointment.

ENDING YOUR POSTS WITH A STRONG CALL TO ACTION

Motivating people to do something may be one of the hardest parts of content marketing, but it is also one of the most important. A call to action is what you use to persuade your clients and prospects to take some type of action on your website. Good calls to action, or CTAs, are precise, easy, and urgent.

USE PRECISE LANGUAGE

The first thing you need to do is decide what you want your viewers to do. Our FMG websites include an option to add a "Contact Us" form on different pages of your website. This is one form of action, but depending on your practice, others may be more appropriate. For example, if you are trying to increase traffic on your blog, you could encourage your viewers to share or comment on your content.

Regardless of what your call to action is, make it very clear to the viewer. Use precise language that explains exactly what the action is. Some examples may include:

- Call Us Today
- Sign Up for Our Monthly Newsletter
- Share on LinkedIn/Facebook/Twitter
- Schedule a First Meeting

Although these calls to action are very different, they all have one thing in common: it is clear what the individual should do.

MAKE IT CLICKABLE

This is more of a design tip, but make sure that your call to action is clickable and easy to access. If your contact form asks individuals to provide their name and email, it should be simple for them to populate these fields and for you to receive the information. You can also add multiple social media buttons on your website for users to follow you. This is a great example of a call to action that is simple and clickable.

MAKE IT EASY

There are few things more counterproductive than a complicated call to action. You want your users to take action, but if that action is too difficult, you won't get very far. For example, if a contact form has too many fields to fill out, chances are the majority of people will give up. Contrarily, if the form only has users fill in their name and email, it will be much easier.

Likewise, the call to action shouldn't request too much of someone. As a general rule, it should only include one or two steps. After that, people lose interest.

GIVE AN INCENTIVE

How does a client or prospect benefit from doing what you are telling them to do? What do they get out of the deal? Viewers are going to be more likely to take action if there is something in it for them. This could be showcasing what you include in your newsletter or a free first meeting. If possible, include a "first customer only" deal.

CREATE URGENCY

Creating a sense of urgency is an age-old marketing technique that you can take advantage of with your calls to action. Our experience shows that people don't want to miss out on a limited-time deal, which will motivate them. Some examples include:

- Take advantage of this limited-time sale today
- Our promotion is ending soon. Act now!
- Sign up for next month's newsletter before it's released

There are countless ways to craft a call to action, but the goal is simple: motivate your viewers to do something!

SE — OH, NO

We can't have a chapter all about websites without mentioning the elephant in the room: Search Engine Optimization (or SEO). I often hear advisors talk about how discouraged they are with their SEO efforts. Either they paid big bucks to work with an SEO company that promised them impossible results, or they tried to incorporate SEO into their site themselves and find themselves on the 36,000th page of a Google Search. With a little work, though, these aren't the only options.

YOUR WEBSITE IS YOUR HUB

Think of your content strategy as a wheel. Your website is in the center, and the other content you send out are the spokes. Although they are their own entity, they all drive back to a central location.

The more educational, quality content you send out to your email contacts, social profiles, or blog, the more routes a visitor has to drive back to your site. When I ride my motorcycle to Duluth, Minnesota (which is quite the trip!), I don't take the same route every time. Sometimes, I take the scenic route, which takes about 10 days, and sometimes I just want to breeze by and take the highway. Giving your clients and prospects multiple ways to get to your website will increase engagement rates without the use of any fancy SEO tools.

CHOOSING KEYWORDS

Keywords are words or phrases that frequently appear within your website and that people will search for in a search engine. In relation to SEO, a good keyword density is between 2 and 4%, meaning your select keywords make up 2 to 4% of your total content. While there are no guarantees in the world of SEO, the goal of incorporating select keywords into your website and content is to help you appear higher in search engine results when someone searches for an advisor in your geographical region or area of specialty.

You want at least 3 and no more than 10. More keywords doesn't necessarily mean more search results. You need a good balance of quality and quantity.

Narrow down your list to your specialties and location. Avoid too technical of jargon, but be specific enough that your prospects will be able to find your site.

TEN MINUTES TODAY

Jot down a list of 5 to 20 words or phrases that come to mind when you think about your practice and what you do. Think of both general terms, like "financial planning," and specific terms, like "IRA Rollover San Diego, CA."

Narrow down your list to your specialties and location. Avoid too technical of jargon, but be specific enough that your prospects will be able to find your site.

Incorporating keywords into your content and producing quality content will help with your search engine results. Google's algorithm is always changing, and you can't expect to be on the first page when someone searches for "financial planning," but these steps will help demystify some of the questions advisors face with SEO. As a summary, some techniques that may work are:

- Including your company name on your homepage
- Mentioning your community
- Offering social share buttons
- Maintaining a blog that is attached to your website, instead of a stand-alone blog
- Registering with local search engines, like Google Places
- Compelling content that drives back to your site

We're not saying don't focus your energy on SEO efforts, but we are saying to approach it a little differently than you might have in the past.

MAKE IT HAPPEN

We've gone over the big picture website trends, changes you can make to your website today, and the importance of understanding what SEO is and isn't. Here are five things you can do to freshen up your site:

1. Review your current website and see how it stacks up with current trends. Do you have too many elements on your site? Is it mobile-responsive?

2. Incorporate personalized content and photos into your website. Focus your attention on your biography and homepage.

3. Use share buttons, forms, and calls to action on every page. Remember, your website should serve as an active lead generation tool.

4. Offer useful, timely content that builds trust and credibility. Your website is the first step in building your brand.

5. Use your website during meetings with prospects and clients in your office and while on the phone. Refer to it often in conversations and talk it up.

Your participation on social media can lead to more connections, more clients, and better communication.

CHAPTER 6:

SIMPLIFYING SOCIAL MEDIA

Along with having a website, social media is the greatest marketing trend I've seen financial advisors embrace in the last few years. According to a Putnam Investments study, more than 81% of financial advisors now use social media for business purposes.[23] I would say the biggest reason for adopting this trend is because of how much success advisors have seen from social media. Of those 81% of advisors using social media, 79% have acquired new clients through social media, with the average annual asset gain standing at $4.6 million.

In a CNBC article, CFP® professional Eric Roberge reported gaining 21 new clients in the 17 months since he started actively blogging and using social media. He shared with CNBC that his success was due to "spreading myself across the Internet. I just started writing my blog, and that created everything else." After creating his articles, he repurposes them for social media and newsletters to keep the buzz going.

I would say that one of the biggest reasons for Eric's success is that he uses each social media platform for different purposes. His Facebook Business page serves as a "public hub for [his] thoughts, writings, and activities"; he uses Twitter to communicate with fellow advisors; and on LinkedIn, he networks with his target client base.[24]

In 2014, when I wrote the first edition of this book, 67% of Americans were on social media. Within just 2 years, that number jumped to 78%.[25] And it's not just teenagers on social media. More than half of Baby Boomers are on social media, and retirees age 65 and older are the fastest-growing group of social networking site users.[26] Even more attractive to financial advisors is the large number of wealthy investors who use social media: a whopping 74%.[27]

THE EVER-EVOLVING NATURE OF SOCIAL MEDIA

Financial advisors know the vast majority of investors use social media, which is why they are utilizing these tools as well. The big question for financial advisors today is not why or how they should join social media, it's how to stay up to date with the latest changes and simplify their strategies to save time. Before we dive into how you can make the most of your time and efforts using social media, let's take a moment to review some of the biggest changes to the most popular social media platforms.

BY THE NUMBERS

More than 90% of marketers indicated that their social media efforts have generated more exposure for their businesses. The second major benefit was increased traffic, with **77% reporting positive results**. Meanwhile, **69% of marketers are utilizing social media** to develop loyal fans and gain marketplace intelligence.[28]

LINKEDIN

LinkedIn is the most professional of the social media platforms. When people aren't using the platform to job hunt, they're using it to consume information in the form of LinkedIn publications — the biggest update to the site in the last few years. LinkedIn launched its very own publishing platform in 2014. At first, only a select few thought leaders could share posts. The platform later extended to all users. These articles are not only more engaging than your standard update post, but they are also incredibly SEO-friendly, appearing in Google searches just as a news article would. I've seen many advisors use LinkedIn's publishing platform to establish their expertise, define their specialty, and target the audience with whom they most want to work. In Chapter 7, we'll explore LinkedIn and how you can use the publishing platform to your advantage.

FACEBOOK

Facebook's user base has vastly changed since it first launched. While first intended for college students, today, the fastest-growing demographics of users are women and people age 55 and older.[29] Facebook is also the most popular social media platform for Baby Boomers, as they largely use the site to stay in touch with family. Among Millennials, Facebook is used as their top news source. When combined, you can see how Facebook has now become the top platform to balance personal posts with newsworthy shares. Videos and images perform much stronger than

TALK THE TALK

PROFILE:
Where visitors are directed when they search your name on a social media site. It includes your name, photo, and any customization you add to it. A profile is different than a page, as a page is typically for a business, like a Facebook page for your firm.

TIMELINE/NEWS FEED:
The log display of updates of all of the people you are connected to. Also called a news feed, the timeline is the first thing you see when you log in to a social network.

POST:
An update on your social media sites. On Facebook and LinkedIn, the length of posts is not limited, but on Twitter, each post is limited to 140 characters.

CREDENTIALS:
Your username, password, and other login information for social sites.

text posts. In fact, text posts have become nearly obsolete. In order for an advisor's post to stand out in someone's feed, visual elements are a must. In Chapter 8, we'll focus on strategies for Facebook.

TWITTER

Twitter has remained surprisingly consistent over the years and has solidified itself as the platform for micro-snippets of information and trending topics. While the use of hashtags has extended to Facebook and other social sites, they're still most important on Twitter, as this community thrives on news and current events. The best way to get your content to stand out in an endless scrolling news feed is to jump on the hashtag train and comment on the latest news. While you'll largely use Facebook and LinkedIn to communicate with a cozier community of people you know, Twitter is your opportunity to interact with people you don't know or wouldn't normally interact with. In Chapter 9, we'll talk more about how an advisor may use this site.

TIME: THE BIGGEST SOCIAL MEDIA HURDLE

There's no beating around the bush: social media marketing is time-consuming. It requires strategy, creativity, responsiveness, and constant evolution. On a weekly basis, 64% of marketers spend 6 or more hours on social media, 41% spend 11 or more hours, and 19% spend more than 20 hours.[30] That's a lot of time to devote to social media alone.

Financial advisors don't have the time marketers do to dedicate to social media. And since financial advisors are in business to help people with their finances (and not to be a marketer), they also may not share the same passion marketers have for social media. Yet they know that building a social network, communicating with followers, and consistently posting is an essential component of marketing. Herein lies the hurdle advisors face.

This is where technology comes into play, solving about 75% of an advisor's social media woes. Curation tools and apps make it easier for you to post on social media consistently and regularly. Let's look at some of the most helpful tools you can use:

AUTOMATION PLATFORM

The simplest way to cut down on your social media content creation is to use evergreen content created by a third party. Evergreen content will always apply to your audience, so it establishes a great baseline for your social media.

As mentioned in Chapter 4, FMG Suite's Content Library is composed entirely of evergreen content on interesting, engaging, and fresh financial topics. It's content you don't have to create or update as time passes. Through FMG Suite's platform, you can automatically send out these evergreen content pieces on your social media profiles. I recommend doing this two to three times per week.

POST SCHEDULER

A social media scheduler is essential for publishing and sharing posts on your social media profiles. Rather than send out your curated and custom posts at various times throughout your day, schedule a week's or month's worth of posts all in one sitting to save time. We suggest you allocate time on a Monday morning to schedule all the posts for that week. This saves you the hassle later on in the week when you will likely be busy with other tasks. Things come up, of course, and you may have to make changes to your schedule, but this way you will have a steady foundation for your posts.

Buffer and Hootsuite are the two most popular social media schedulers. You can manually post or allow the program to post for you at the best time. Depending on your account level, you can also access analytics to review what posts performed best.

CONTENT CURATION APP

Similar to evergreen content, curated content will make up around one-third of your posts. Instead of sorting through multiple news sites and publications, a curation tool makes it easier to find content most relevant to your audience. My personal favorite is *Flipboard*, because it is easy to use and you can specify what content you want to see. The app has categories such as personal finance, funding news, and the stock market bubble. By choosing just the categories that are relevant, I can quickly sift through news, articles, videos, and blogs that are generated just for me and choose which ones make sense to share on my social media.

TEN MINUTES TODAY

Have you got 10 minutes to spare? Download a content curation app, such as Flipboard, and create your own collection of articles about digital marketing, business practices, or whatever you find helpful. If you spend 10 minutes a day reviewing this information, you will garner great new ideas and you'll stay current with trends.

Another great curation tool is Pocket. Pocket helps users curate content by providing a platform for users to save content they find on the Internet all in one place. Pocket keeps all of your interesting images, articles, and videos in one place for reference. You can group items by tagging, and built-in search functionality makes finding those articles easy. Ditch the laundry list of bookmarks and links in your email inbox and turn to Pocket to curate these useful articles for later reference when you have time.

POST RECYCLER

In Chapter 4, I discussed the frustratingly short lifecycle of content, particularly on social media. Within a few hours, your post will have reached about half of its total audience. That means a lot of people are missing out on seeing your content. You can cut back on the content you have to create and curate by recycling and reposting some of your favorite and top-performing pieces.

Once you've been curating and creating content for a while, it's easy to forget about your older posts that are still relevant and that you can re-share. *Edgar* is an easy tool that reposts content from your archive onto your social media channels, helping you drive new traffic to your site and breathe new life to the content you've worked hard to create and curate. The great thing about this tool is that it kills two birds with one stone: it helps you squeeze more juice out of your content and makes it easier to keep your social media profiles active with frequent postings.

FOLLOW AN EDITORIAL CALENDAR

An editorial calendar is a high-level calendar that will outline your content for your social media pages. I recommend you start with your automated content, filling in the scheduled posts. From there you can start to pencil in what you will be posting for the week or month. Then, use a scheduler platform to schedule your posts. This approach might seem daunting at first, but I think you will see the benefits and discover just how much time you can save in the end. Here are a few a reasons to support this:

- **Branding**
  Creating an editorial calendar allows you to choose a focus for your profiles. Whether it is retirement or 401(k)s that you want to talk about, all of this will be in line with your brand and what you are emphasizing in your other marketing channels.

- **Organization**
  An editorial calendar will help you keep your social profiles organized. You won't have to wonder if you've already posted a link, or if you have sent attendees the link to your next client appreciation meeting.

- **Time**
  An editorial calendar will allow you to save time. At the

beginning of each week, sitting down and creating the posts for the week will ease the stress of feeling like you have to dedicate huge chunks of your time to your profiles every day.

Once you have established an editorial calendar, it will be easy to get your staff involved. Having a secretary or office administrator spend time monitoring your social media will be one of the easiest ways to ensure your success. Add social media to the agenda in your office meetings, just as you would the other aspects of your marketing. We'll talk more in-depth about how to create an editorial calendar for your social media marketing in Chapter 10.

SET A TIME LIMIT FOR EACH TASK

As we are all aware, it's easy to get adrift in the sea of the Internet and quickly get buried in responses, to-do lists, and research. It may help to set a time limit for each social media task and set an alarm to remind you when it's time to switch gears. Your schedule could look something like this:

- 2 hours per month curating content from Flipboard or your favorite publications.
- 2 hours per month creating your editorial calendar.
- 1 hour scheduling posts for the month.
- 15 minutes every few days responding to followers.
- 15 minutes every few days finding and connecting with prospects, clients, and acquaintances.
- 1 hour every 3 to 6 months updating your profiles, including adding a new headshot or cover photos, updating your credentials, or changing any information.

Following this timetable can help you feel less overwhelmed by the amount of work that has to be done for an effective social media strategy. Use your calendar to schedule posts for the month, take time at the beginning of the week or month to make your next set of posts, and monitor your daily time on social media. You'll be your own social media manager in no time.

Too often, financial advisors get tied up in the numbers aspect of social media, believing their profile's worth is based on how many likes or followers they have. While these facets are helpful to gauge the growth of your profiles and the successes of specific posts, it's not the end all, be all. Marketing experts know that "vanity metrics" are extremely common in the world of content marketing, but can actually be unhelpful and inaccurate. It doesn't do you much good to have 10,000 Twitter followers if only 10 of them are prospective clients and the rest are spam or random accounts.

Whether you want clients to sign up for your email newsletter, follow your blog, or contact your office to schedule an appointment, your social media strategy should act as a way to encourage engagement, not merely to rack up fans. A simple way to encourage action on your social media platforms is to express clearly what you want your viewers to do. For example, if you share an article about the rising cost of automobile insurance, ask your viewers to contact your office to learn more about how you can help. Ultimately, you want your strategy to help you get clients and prospects to take action, not just "like," "share," or "retweet" your post.

MAKE IT HAPPEN

Social media marketing is a fundamental component of an efficient inbound marketing strategy. It is important, however, to capture the right "voice" on your social media sites. Sure, you want people to know that you are a serious professional with all the expertise necessary to help them with their financial decisions, but that is not all that you want to accomplish. You also want potential clients to get to know you personally, and feel that they can trust you. Social media offers an opportunity to do both, but only if you strike the right balance on each of your sites.

Here are two steps to take to strengthen your social media profiles:

1. **Decide on a definite focus for each of your sites**

   My suggestion is to let your Facebook Business page be the place where you show charitable work, personal interests, and even family news items from you and your staff members, as well as events in your community. Load your LinkedIn profile with more professional financial information. Twitter is a great place to link to interesting articles, quotes, and news reports that may impact your followers.

2. **Post something, somewhere, every day**

   Don't let weeks slip by without adding fresh content to your profiles or people will simply stop visiting. There are many ways to schedule posts and tweets in advance so that you don't have to think about it several times a day. And remember that you can link to an article, video or another piece of content in a variety of posts and tweets. Aim to post something on any one of your platforms once per weekday.

CHAPTER 7:

LINK UP ON LINKEDIN

A few years ago while reaching out to current clients on LinkedIn, I came across Ron Carson, President of Carson Wealth Management Group and Founder of Peak Advisor Alliance. I had met Ron almost 20 years earlier but we had lost touch. I was interested in what Ron was doing and thought there might be an opportunity for us to collaborate, so I sent him a personal message on LinkedIn, asking him to connect with me. I didn't realize that Ron had been noticing our work at FMG Suite and had been thinking along the same lines. When he saw my message, he picked up the phone.

One thing led to another and together we created "Digital Fortress," a complete practice management program for advisors under the Peak umbrella. Thanks to LinkedIn, our collaboration has reached thousands of advisors, increased the number of users on the platform, and opened us up to new industry opportunities through the relationships we have built.

In the last few years, LinkedIn has undergone some major transformations, making it one of the most preferred social media sites for financial advisors. Their improved user experience, publishing platform, and vast reach make it a great place to put your best foot forward. LinkedIn reaches more than 433 million users worldwide,[31] and is responsible for 64% of all visits from social media channels to corporate websites.[32]

In this chapter, I'll show you how to make your LinkedIn profile stand out, the importance of publishing updates and posts, how to get involved with LinkedIn groups, and advertising opportunities on LinkedIn.

YOU'RE PROBABLY MAKING THIS LINKEDIN PROFILE MISTAKE

I don't want to be the bearer of bad news, but I suspect that you are guilty of making the biggest mistake on LinkedIn. The reason I think this? Because I was guilty of it, too, once.

As a professional marketer, I like to think that I have it all figured out. Blogging, check. Facebook posts, check. LinkedIn, check? LinkedIn first launched in 2002 as a place where jobseekers and companies could connect on the Internet. It made sense, then, to make your LinkedIn profile read like a virtual resume. Most users laid out their experience, education, certifications, and other things that would help them get a job. Simply put, it was all about you. Even in the first edition of *The Art of Inbound Marketing*, we talked about how to write a dynamic summary and list your specialties effectively. While some of these techniques can still be used throughout your profile, you may want to reconsider how you approach your profile.

THE MISTAKE

Fast forward to more than 13 years after LinkedIn's inception. It seems absurd to treat social networks the same as we did when they first launched, but for most of our LinkedIn profiles, that is exactly what we're doing. Your LinkedIn profile likely reads like a resume, is focused on yourself, and lacks dynamism.

While your credentials and work experience are undoubtedly impressive, clients and prospects care more about how you can offer value and solve their problems.

THE SOLUTION

Instead of having your LinkedIn profile serve as your online resume, you should make it focused on how you can help a specific, target audience achieve their goals. Why should a client or prospect choose to work with you over your competitors?

The good news is that the answer to this question is usually pretty clear for financial advisors. It's likely that you serve a specific market, such as pre-retirees and those living in retirement, and help them with specific concerns, such as supplementing their income, learning about low-risk investments, or planning for their legacy.

Start with the Summary section on your LinkedIn profile. Your summary should answer a few questions:

- What do you you do and what are your specialties?
- With whom do you work?
- How do you help your clientele solve their problems?
- What makes you different?

Here is an example:

I help women achieve financial empowerment by providing a safe space for them to ask their questions. I partner with leading attorneys and accountants to provide a holistic financial planning experience. My planning process is different than others because I meet with my clients in their homes and don't talk over their heads. If you would like to get started, contact my office at 555-555-5555.

This is a very simple example, but you can tell how client-centric it is. It talks about what this advisor does, with whom they work, and how they help. It doesn't go into detail about the advisor's experience (which can be somewhere else on the profile), but instead focuses on the benefits of working with them.

Let's compare that to another profile with a great summary. Kathryn Phillips lets us know in just a few accomplishment-driven statements what she does and what we can expect from her, using phrases that contain keywords that would be used in a Google search. Most importantly, she highlights what type of client she is looking to work with. She does this by confidently stating what she can offer potential clients. Notice that she's not afraid to let you know exactly how she does business. Take a look:

Phillips Investment Group is an investment advisory firm. We specialize in assisting affluent couples who would like to effectively manage their finances together as well as single women who may be going through a life transition such as divorce, widowhood, or retirement.

Each of our advisors has more than two decades of experience as financial advisors and wealth managers. Together, we have helped hundreds of men and women with portfolios over $1 million manage their finances during times of transition.

I serve locally with three nonprofits dedicated to women's financial independence. I also contribute regularly to financialplanning. com and other trade publications. As co-author of the book, Your Money, Your Life, I am an advocate for more comprehensive financial education and speak regularly on topics related to women and money.

Specialties: Comprehensive Financial Planning, Retirement Planning, Divorce, Widowhood & Retirement Portfolio Management, Securities License in OH, NJ, FL, TX, PR

Visit our website for investment tips and market updates: www. phillipsinvestmentgroup.com.

In addition to your summary and experience, LinkedIn offers a multitude of other opportunities to shine. Spend time uploading a professional headshot, filling in your education and certifications, and making sure everything looks presentable. You would be surprised at how many advisors I connect with on LinkedIn that haven't created a presentable profile. And if you don't believe me, the numbers don't lie! Adding a professional headshot makes you 14 times more likely to be found on LinkedIn.[33]

In this well-written summary, she:

- Clearly lists her specialties
- Describes her ideal client
- Uses accomplishment-driven statements (Two decades of experience…)
- Highlights her qualifications (co-author)
- Tells her story (serves locally)
- Uses keywords (retirement, divorce, single women)
- Ends with a call to action

Take a cue from Kathryn and be specific rather than try to be everything to everyone. Give them an accurate idea of what to expect with your summary. Your summary does not need to be lengthy, but it should be well written. Don't hesitate to ask for help in writing something that represents you.

LinkedIn is an opportunity to create a professional, confident, and competent environment that will build your business. In addition to creating a profile, LinkedIn has many ways to connect to clients and prospects, including publishing both short- and long-form posts and various advertising opportunities.

TALK THE TALK

SHORT-FORM CONTENT: *Content that is created rather quickly and is intended to be consumed by the viewer just as fast. Examples include tweets, status updates, infographics, and even short blog posts and articles (under 350 words).*

LONG-FORM CONTENT: *In-depth content designed to give its audience a large amount of detail and information and includes things like ebooks, whitepapers, and long blog post series.*

A few years ago, LinkedIn served as a place where users could post short updates about their company or personal endeavors and these posts would be shared, similar to tweets and Facebook statuses, to their Connections. But in February 2014, LinkedIn changed its publishing platform to allow all users (not just Influencers) to post long-form content. You can now use LinkedIn to post regular updates, comment on other users' posts, and post your own articles.

LINKEDIN UPDATES

LinkedIn Updates are the short updates that you are probably used to seeing most often. These posts usually include industry insights and company news. Adding visuals, posting consistently, and keeping your updates short are great ways to stay ahead of the curve when it comes to utilizing LinkedIn.

LET'S GET VISUAL

When posting, remember the visual rules of social media. Images posted get a 98% higher comment rate, and sharing a YouTube video garners a 75% higher share rate.[34] Users love to see visual aspects with text posts, so think about the image you want to add when drafting your updates. When sharing an article from an outside source, make sure a thumbnail is attached, or add your own.

CONSISTENCY IS KEY

As with other social media platforms, posting consistently on LinkedIn is a great way to stay top-of-mind with your clients and prospects. According to LinkedIn,[35] posting 20 updates a month allows you to reach 60% of your audience. While this may not be a feasible goal for some financial advisors, the important part is creating a cadence that works for you and sticking with it. Automated scheduling tools may help you plan posts out in advance and schedule them regularly.

SHORT AND SWEET

Updates can be about an upcoming office event, a change in hours, or a recent article that is relevant to your firm with a short comment. To prevent your posts from getting cut off and to ensure they display correctly, keep the title under 70 characters, and the link description under 250 characters.

PUBLISHING POSTS

Being able to publish longer posts is a relatively new feature for LinkedIn. Before the launch of their publishing platform in February 2014, only influencers, or famous users, were able to publish longer posts. Fortunately, now all users can post long-form content. This means that LinkedIn can serve as your professional profile, hub of publications, *and* blog. Published posts can drive viewers back to your website, as well.

HOW TO POST

First, before we dive into the benefits of publishing posts on LinkedIn, let's explain how to post. After creating a personal LinkedIn profile, go to your homepage. At the top, you should see a few options, such as "Share an Update," "Upload a Photo," and "Publish a Post." Click "Publish a Post."

You will be taken to a page that prompts you to add an image, headline, and text. You can use a previously published blog post or write something new!

WHAT TO POST

Figuring out what to post is the million dollar question when it comes to social media marketing. There are infinite possibilities, and yet it may seem impossible to start. Let's look at one financial advisor, Sean, who seems to have nailed down how to post successfully.

At the time of writing, Sean has over 1,600 followers (in addition to his 500+ LinkedIn connections) and a regular stream of posts, including posting at least once a month. He writes about topics including robo-advisors, financial tips, and retirement planning. His posts are engaging and interesting. And best of all, they can easily be shared with his followers' friends and family!

PRO TIP:
Mike Woods, Vice President of Compliance and Content at FMG Suite

There are a few compliance concerns to be aware of with LinkedIn, so we asked our compliance guru to weigh in on the issue. As always, check with your home office's compliance department first to confirm their compliance guidelines before moving forward on any social network.

Are advisors allowed to receive recommendations on LinkedIn profiles?
LinkedIn recommendations are considered an endorsement, which is a big "no no." After all, an advisor could create 10 imaginary friends and have them all give glowing endorsements.

When publishing posts, what should advisors consider with compliance?
As with other marketing materials, LinkedIn published posts must be approved by compliance or archived by a social software. To be sure, check with your home office before launching your social campaign.

Is there anything else an advisor would want to know when setting up a LinkedIn profile?
All of this is a firm by firm decision. That's the key. FINRA sets the guidelines but it's up to the individual firm to implement them. Generally, firms will error on the "conservative interpretation" of any FINRA rule. For example, if FINRA says keep records for three years, most firms keep records for four years.

FINRA says social media must be treated as other forms of advertisements and communication with the public. Firms will apply their most strict rules to social media to feel compliant. Remember, FINRA may fine firms if they believe the firm or the firm's reps didn't follow established guidelines.

A few things that Sean does well: He writes about the topics he knows the most about, addresses his target audience, and establishes himself as a knowledgeable source on a few salient topics rather than trying to be a jack-of-all-trades.

Here are some questions to think about when deciding what to write:

- What will the financial services industry look like in 5, 10, or 15 years?
- What is the biggest problem you solve for your clients?
- What advice would you give someone looking to become an independent financial advisor?
- How has the financial industry changed since you began your career?
- What are some of the main challenges for the future of financial professionals?

My guess is that even just skimming these questions jogs some ideas. Being a financial advisor is a profession that changes rapidly and with the rise of robo-advisors, fiduciary changes, emerging markets, and many more, there is always a new topic to write about. Let's lay out how you would start a post that addresses the last question above: "What are some of the main challenges for the future of financial professionals?"

First, gather your research. Dig deep into what various financial publications and websites are focusing on, conduct short interviews with your team members and colleagues, and reflect on your own experiences. You don't need a lot of research and might want to start with enough to craft one or two LinkedIn posts.

Next, lay out how you want to tackle the subject. Do you want to address three or four main challenges and give a brief overview of each? Do you want to go into more detail about one change, and expand on the others in later posts? These are questions that you must answer according to your content marketing goals because there is no one right or wrong answer.

Think about the tone you want to convey. LinkedIn is a professional social media site, which means that you should avoid posting anything obscene, shocking, hateful, or otherwise unprofessional. Don't be afraid to express your opinion, but keep your writing focused, authentic, and thoughtful. Lastly, proofread, add some images and hyperlinks to your post, and create a schedule that will help you post consistently!

BECOME A LINKEDIN GROUPIE

LinkedIn groups are like clubs within LinkedIn, centered around an industry or a topic. There are thousands of these groups and the number of people in a group ranges from five to 50,000. Some of them are completely open to the public, while others are fairly exclusive and require acceptance by the head of the group.

Members start conversations on the group's message board and then chime in when they have something to say regarding the topic. For example, the Financial Planning Magazine group offers an ongoing conversation between advisors about topics of interest.

The most common way to use LinkedIn groups is as an opportunity to network with professionals and thought leaders in your own industry. There are some great financial groups out there, including Financial Advisor Network, which has over 8,000 members; Independent Financial Advisors, which has over 4,600 members; and hundreds more. These groups focus on business-building ideas and cater to financial professionals.

MORE ONLINE

Join our LinkedIn group "*Digital Marketing For Financial Professionals*". This group is open to financial advisors to discuss and share how they successfully incorporate digital marketing into their practice.

USING GROUPS AS A PROSPECTING TOOL

One way to generate business from LinkedIn is to search for groups that are relevant to the markets you serve. For example, if you work with those preparing for or living in retirement, try searching for groups that have the word "retired" in them. Now, filter the groups so you only search for ones that are open to the public. Select a few that are of interest to you and join them!

What you'll find is that people in these groups are starting conversations and posing questions about money, Social Security, and other topics that a financial professional could help with. And that financial professional should be you! By offering industry insight and tips, you'll build relationships and leads right away. Don't forget that this is LinkedIn — people are here for business-related reasons, so don't pass up the opportunity to network and hunt for prospects by offering information.

ADVERTISING ON LINKEDIN

In addition to using LinkedIn to grow your social media presence, it is also a good platform for financial advisors that are interested in paid advertisements. There are different forms of advertisements on LinkedIn, including pay-per-click advertisements, sponsored InMail, and sponsored updates. Let's look at some of the most common types of ads and how you can get started advertising on social media.

1. PAY-PER-CLICK ADS

These ads are similar to what you generally see in search engines like Google, including banner and sidebar ads. For these kinds of ads, you can either specify the amount you want to pay every time someone clicks your ad, or the amount you want to pay per 1,000 impressions of your ad, meaning the amount of times someone sees your ad (not how many times it's clicked).

Pay-per-click, or PPC, ads are useful for service professionals who want to generate traffic back to their website and don't have a lot of content to post for sponsored ads. One benefit of PPC ads is that you can create multiple versions of an ad and see which do the best.

2. SPONSORED INMAIL

Sponsored InMail allows companies to send InMail messages to targeted audiences. InMail has always been a good way for service professionals to connect with their current clients and prospects, and Sponsored InMail allows them to message a targeted audience they may not have interacted with before.

For example, if you are hosting a retirement planning seminar, you may want to use Sponsored InMail to send a message to LinkedIn users that are in your target age range, either nearing or in retirement, and who live in your local area.

3. SPONSORED CONTENT

One of the best parts of social media is that users are able to publish and share their own, and their network's, content. LinkedIn has utilized this social aspect and has Sponsored Content, which allows companies to share an update to people outside of their network. With this type of ad, your post will appear in the homepage feed of targeted users.

Sponsored Content ads are a good option for service professionals that post relevant, unique content worth sharing. The premise is that your sponsored post will entice users to click on your profile and learn more about your company.

There are other forms of advertisements on LinkedIn, but there are the ones that may be most appropriate for financial advisors and other service professionals. Remember, before starting a LinkedIn ad campaign, you will need a LinkedIn Business profile and a LinkedIn advertising account.

If you don't have one already, create a LinkedIn profile right now. It is as easy as putting in your email address and basic information.

1. Go to LinkedIn.com. Click "Join Today."

2. You will be asked to provide your first name, last name, an email address, and a password. Make sure to use a business email address you check regularly because you will have to verify it.

3. Verify your email address if necessary, fill in any other prompts, and you should be set! You can then start adding personal details, like the client-facing Summary and Work Experience we explained earlier, any skills and certifications you have, and a headshot.

After you make your profile, play around on LinkedIn and see what you can discover. Join a group, publish a post, or find people you know to connect with! With some time and dedication, you'll be a social media pro in no time.

CHAPTER 8:

FACING THE FACEBOOK FACTS

A few years ago, I took a 2,700-mile motorcycle trip across the country from our San Diego headquarters to our development team's office in Duluth, Minnesota. At various stops along the way, I filmed marketing tips with my GoPro and took photos of the local area. It was an amazing trip for me, and social media helped it double as a great work opportunity, as I sprinkled in some marketing tips and industry insights to my social media posts along the way.

I invited colleagues and clients to follow my trip and post comments and, as a result, saw a substantial increase in my Facebook following. The fun, upbeat content resonated with people and gave them a glimpse into how we do things here at FMG Suite.

Facebook gives you an opportunity, such as this, to showcase your personality and what makes you unique, both personally and professionally.

IT'S NOT IF; IT'S HOW

Facebook is the largest social network and attracts users of all ages, including Millennials, working professionals, and those ready to retire. Worldwide, there are over 1.65 billion monthly active Facebook users, with an average 15% increase year over year.[36] Today, 71% of adult Internet users and 58% of the entire adult population use Facebook, and the 65+ age group is the fastest growing on the network.[37]

At this stage in the social media marketing game, we know it isn't about convincing you to be on Facebook, because you likely know the benefits. Rather, our goal is to explain some of the network's best practices, how to make the most out of your social media marketing, and share what other advisors are doing well.

MORE ONLINE

For a quick training video that walks you through each step for setting up your Facebook Business page, visit FMG Suite's blog.

CREATING A FACEBOOK BUSINESS PAGE

There are some key differences between personal and professional Facebook pages. Users dedicate their personal profile to sharing intimate moments in their lives with people they know, while a Facebook Business page is a professional way to display information to clients and prospects.

You can start a Facebook Business page in four easy steps.

1. Log onto your personal Facebook page, click the arrow in the top-right corner, and select "Create Page."

2. Choose a business category for your page. You can choose from options such as public figure, product, or institution. Most of our clients will fall under local business.

3. Next, you will choose an industry that is appropriate for your page, fill in some information about your business, and get started!

4. Once you create your page, add as much information as possible, including your address, phone number, website URL, and other information. Upload a headshot or your logo for your profile image (which should be a square image that is at least 180 x 180 pixels). For your cover image (which should be 851 x 315 pixels), add a picture of your location, your office, or another image from your website for consistency.

Here's a great example of an advisor's Facebook Business page.

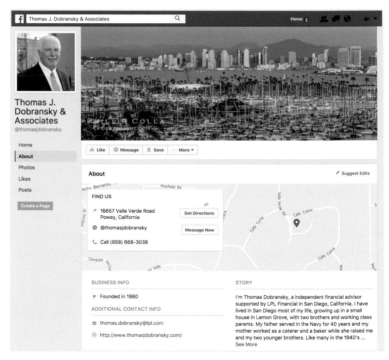

Now that you have your information on your Business page, invite your clients and friends to "like" it. While the number of likes on your page isn't the ultimate tell-all of your social media marketing success, it is something to consider and spend time cultivating.

In addition to promoting your Business page organically, Facebook offers different advertising options that you might want to consider.

CRAIG'S SECRET FOR SUCCESS

Think carefully about the photos and videos that fill out your page. You may want to include a few pictures of your geographical area, your personal interests, or members of your staff. This is what our VP of Content and Creative Services, Brandon Brown, calls "information-rich" photography. Let people know who you are and, right from the start, create an environment that will encourage them to return to your page.

READY, SET, POST!

Every social media platform has its own suggestions and best practices when posting content. LinkedIn is mostly professional posts, Twitter's updates are short and to the point, and Facebook falls somewhere in between. Often, advisors shy away from posting too many company updates on Facebook because they think of it as a merely personal platform. As explained earlier, Facebook can be both a personal and professional outlet.

⏱ EVERY MINUTE ON FACEBOOK...

📺 510 comments are posted

💬 293,000 statuses are updated

🖼 136,000 photos are uploaded

Source: Zephoria

One of FMG Suite's users, Bair Financial Planning, does a great job with their social media strategy on Facebook. They post an effective mix of evergreen content (such as videos from FMG's Content Library), curated posts that relate to their niche market, and original posts. For example, they received a gift basket from a client and posted a picture and thank you note. While it only took a few seconds to write, posts like these do wonders for social marketing and show that the firm goes the extra mile.

Beyond personal photos and evergreen content, let's look a little further at the types of posts that perform best on Facebook:

QUOTES

Everyone loves a good quote, whether it's funny or inspiring. Rather than just post a quote in text form, use an image version. You can create this in a few minutes using a photo editing program, such as Photoshop, or an online site, like Canva, to create inexpensive or free images. You can also often find quote images online.

INFOGRAPHICS

Infographics are one of my favorite visual elements for sharing stats-heavy information. As interesting as statistics or facts are, they become boring quickly when you list them out, one after another in a dry format. An infographic allows you to display this information in a fun, colorful, and engaging format. They're highly shareable and a great way to build traction on Facebook.

VIDEOS

Videos see more reach on Facebook than any other type of content.[38] Why? Because everyone loves videos. They're the easiest way to simultaneously learn new information and be entertained, which will always be the prime goal of social media platforms like Facebook.

You may have noticed that text posts did not make the list. It's hard to make a text-only post stand out in an endlessly long feed of cooking videos and cat pictures. You can certainly post content that is largely text-based, but you should try to pair it with an image or video to help it stand out.

In Chapter 4, we covered the basics of posting content, including the types of content (original, evergreen, and curated), different formats that content can take, and the necessities you must know for content success.

For Facebook, I suggest going back and taking notes while reading that chapter, developing a strategy that incorporates different content types, and planning your posts out in advance. There are multiple scheduling programs online, some of which are free or available at a very low cost. I'll let you in on a little secret: at FMG, our marketing team spends time scheduling all of our Facebook posts in the beginning of the month for the next few weeks. We sprinkle timely content in, as well, but the skeleton of our posts is created in advance.

TEN MINUTES TODAY

Go through your content library and plan your Facebook posts for the next two weeks. Sign up for a social scheduling platform like Hootsuite or Buffer and schedule your posts, starting with once a day.

CREATING THE PERFECT FACEBOOK POST

While there's no guarantee a post will go viral, we have learned enough to assemble some guidelines as to what a great, shareable, and action-inspiring post looks like. Here are a few steps to take when creating your Facebook posts:

1. **Keep it Short**
   Posts below 250 characters can see up to 60% more engagement, and posts under 80 characters can garner 66% more engagement.[39]

2. **Include a Link**

   You're not posting on Facebook for the sake of it. Ideally, it's part of a marketing strategy that will result in more business. All of your posts should include a link, whether it's to your website (an inbound method) or to an article on another site (an outbound method).

3. **Feature Visuals**

   We've said it before, so we don't need to say much about it again. Visuals rule Facebook's feed and they're your best bet for gaining likes and shares.

4. **Use Action Words**

   To get someone to take action you have to inspire action. Tell your viewers what you want them to do with your post. Do you want them to share it? Click on the link? Add a comment? Be explicit. For example, if you're hoping to gain comments, ask a question or post a fill-in-the-blank statement. If you want them to download your whitepaper, encourage them to click on your link to receive a free whitepaper.

5. **Be Timely**

   As I said before, you're not posting for the sake of saying something. Everything you post should have a purpose. Before I post something, I like to ask, "Will my audience get something out of it?" Whether it's education or simply a laugh, there should be a reason for every post.

6. **Make it a Part of a Consistent Sharing Strategy**

   The best Facebook Business pages don't just post good content; they post consistently at regular intervals. Avoid posting like crazy for a week and then going dark for the next month. It's better to post three times a week every week than three times in a day once in awhile.

Keep in mind that likes and shares are just one metric for gauging social media metrics. And even though we've talked about them, they're not the most important nor do they determine the success of your strategy. It's easy to fall into the trap of thinking more is better. While yes, you can gain new followers simply because your numbers are impressive, it doesn't mean those new followers match your ideal clientele. I've always said that I'd rather have 100 loyal social media followers who match my ideal client criteria than 10,000 random Internet strangers.

RULES OF THE FACEBOOK ROAD

I trust that because you work with people every day and you have seen the evolution of social media, you know most of the best practices on Facebook (or if you don't, they are common sense). That said, though, I would be remiss if I didn't lay out some of the trends marketers have noticed throughout the last few years, including things to do more of and things to avoid.

DO:

- Mix in original, curated, and evergreen posts.
- Respond to comments and messages in a timely manner. Thank them for taking the time to reach out!
- Participate in conversations with followers by asking questions or asking for feedback.
- Follow relevant accounts, like industry thought leaders and publications.
- Post photos and videos. Content with relevant images gets 94% more views than content without relevant images.[40]

DON'T:

- Post too much. Gauge your audience and think about crafting quality posts.
- Use bad grammar or spelling.
- Overshare. Avoid politics, religion, or any other "hot button" issues.
- Bad mouth others in your industry.
- Share too many personal details on your Business page. Save the intimate details for your close friends and family.

These are just a few of the many social media tips out there, and most of them shouldn't come as too big of a shock. Social media is meant to be fun, engaging, and a place to make new connections. You will know what is best to post for your firm the more you practice.

ADVERTISING ON FACEBOOK

Advertising on Facebook provides the opportunity to reach a targeted audience and generate the specific results you are looking for, and it is much more affordable than traditional advertising techniques. First, let's break down the different forms of advertisements that Facebook offers. Depending on your end goal, you can choose the type of ad that is suitable for your firm.

PAGE POST ENGAGEMENT

Page Post Engagement is an ad that promotes a specific post, either of text or a photo. For example, a financial advisor could share a post of their renovated office, and draw people to their Facebook Business page to gain more likes and comments. This is a good option for advisors that have worked hard on a specific post and want it to get as much exposure as possible.

PAGE LIKES

Business owners use this advertising option to increase the number of likes on their Facebook Business pages. This type of ad is a good option if you want to show off your Facebook page and share insightful, useful content with future followers. It's an excellent opportunity for financial advisors to increase their reach, both at the time and in the future.

CLICKS TO WEBSITE

In this type of ad, the call to action is to visit your website. As with the other forms of advertisements that Facebook offers, you can choose the target audience and demographic you would like to reach. When users click the ad, it goes right to your website. You can direct them to a specific page, such as your services offered, or just to the homepage so they can explore what you're offering.

WEBSITE CONVERSIONS

This ad is a little more complex than the others, because what users can do is alter the code in their website and track user actions, such as entering their email for your newsletter or reaching out to your office. We suggest having a contact form on every page of your website, so this type of ad might not be directly applicable to your practice.

VIDEO VIEWS

Video advertising can be good for businesses that have high-quality videos they think prospective viewers would enjoy. This may be more applicable to big businesses that have a budget to create good videos, but small businesses could benefit from this form of advertising as well.

APP INSTALLS

This is an ad where the call to action is for users to download the business's app. Rather than have a button that says "Like This Page" or "Visit Website," it says "Install Now" and directs users to the app. Keep in mind, this form of advertisement is only shown on mobile devices because users are on their device ready for the download.

OFFER CLAIMS

Offer ads are perfect if you want people to come into your office and have face-to-face interactions with your team. To create an offer, your Business page must have at least 50 likes. Examples of offers may be an aspect of service for free or a discount. Depending on your business structure, this may be a good way to get people in the door.

EVENT RESPONSES

Facebook Events have been around for a while, which is why businesses take advantage of their reach. If you have an event or seminar, this ad may be the best option to promote that event. Marketers can adjust the geographical reach of the ad to attract prospects in the appropriate area.

It should come as no surprise that social media advertising is the future of marketing. It's less expensive, more direct, and easier to track than traditional advertising methods. It's easy to take advantage of the clear ROI, eight billion daily views,[41] and targeted audiences.

MAKE IT HAPPEN ▮▬▬▬▬▬▬▬▬▬▬▬▬▬▬▬▬▬

If you don't have one already, set up a Facebook Business page, which was explained earlier in the chapter. Make sure it's populated with accurate and interesting content.

After creating your page, brainstorm some ideas for this month's posts. Are there any holidays you should acknowledge? Client birthdays or retirements? Industry trends? Think of a post a day for the month.

Sign up for a scheduling software and plug your posts in. Don't forget to add media like videos and pictures to your posts.

After doing this for a few months in a row, analyze the results. Do more of what worked and less of what didn't.

CHAPTER 9:

MAKING TWITTER WORK FOR YOU

There's no getting around it: air travel is often frustrating. Whether you've had to sleep in an airport overnight, missed your connecting flight, or had to sit next to a seat-hogger or snorer, you probably know what I'm talking about. American Airlines knows what I'm talking about, too, and has taken a unique approach to client interactions on social media.

American Airlines is known for using Twitter to field their customer service requests. Customers can tweet them a complaint and their social media team usually responds right away. American Airlines is a large corporation and likely has many more resources to handle social media than you as a small business owner, but their model is a good one. Being active on Twitter is a great way to reinforce your brand, respond to customers instantaneously, and add to your social media footprint.

TALK THE TALK

TWEET:
The posts on Twitter that are 140 characters or less.

HASHTAG:
A word or phrase preceded by a hash or pound sign (#) used to identify messages on a specific topic.

EMOJI:
A small character, such as a person or smiley face, found on the keyboard of most smartphones.

TWITTER LISTS:
A list of users with a common interest, such as online marketers or those living in the same geographical area.

"TO TWEET OR NOT TO TWEET?" THAT IS THE FINANCIAL ADVISOR'S QUESTION

Twitter is the second-largest social network, but its use of symbols and rapid news feed can intimidate many first-time users. I've had many advisors come to me with the same question about Twitter: "It's fine, but what would I do there?" Twitter is not just for Justin Bieber and Ashton Kutcher; there are a growing number of financial professionals having meaningful conversations on the site. Here are three ways Twitter can be a useful and beneficial network for financial advisors.

1. TWITTER IS THE NEW CNN

If you're interested in companies like *Financial Planning*, *The Washington Post*, and *The Economist*, Twitter is a great place to stay current with what these companies are talking about.

For example, if I see from a tweet that Financial Times has recently posted something that I'm interested in, I can easily click the link to check it out. During the day, I can also get market updates from companies like Market Watch, keeping me abreast of everything I would need to know as an advisor to stay informed.

2. THE SECRET OF 140 CHARACTERS

Twitter's messages and tweets are limited to just 140 characters, making updates interesting and quick to send out. Many advisors feel that they don't have time to spend writing lengthy blog posts or social messages during their workday. Twitter solves that problem with their 140 characters.

The secret of Twitter is that through its character limitation, it's easy to share articles and engage in quick conversations. This is encouraging for two reasons. First, you know you can follow other companies' news through easy-to-read posts. Second, you won't have to spend long periods of time crafting your tweets. Additionally, of all the social networks, Twitter is the most conversational. Its short character messages lead to great conversations with potential clients. For that reason, Twitter has become the choice for many companies (like American Airlines) as a marketing tool and customer service platform.

3. TWITTER LISTS: A QUICK WAY TO NETWORK

Twitter lists allow you to group any number of Twitter accounts together. When you go into that list, you will see the most recent posts from the people you have added to list. The list can be created for your public or private use.

For example, you might want to create a private list of people who could be potential clients and check the list for updates from members. You could also create a public list of some of the most influential thought leaders in the financial industry to stay abreast on what the most salient topics are. Twitter lists make sorting through all of the updates really easy and a quick response to these tweets will help build your relationship.

Twitter can be a little intimidating. The key to finding success is creating some lists and not just diving in unprepared. Start to experiment with Twitter. The young, wealthy, college educated individuals are there, and, increasingly, other demographics are jumping in. If you're looking for a platform that helps you stay in touch with industry thought leaders, have real conversations, and easily follow breaking news, Twitter is a great place to be.

PRO TIP:

Twitter and the Financial Professional: A Conversation with Michael Kitces

Michael Kitces is a social media influencer and the publisher of the financial planning blog, *Nerd's Eye View.* In addition, his firm, Pinnacle Advisory Group, manages over $1.3 billion in client assets. Our VP of Marketing and Creative, Brandon Brown, sat down with him to discuss tips on how to reach a wider audience of highly qualified prospects.

Brandon: Why is Twitter an ideal environment for business opportunities?

Michael: I have done pretty much everything on every social media platform out there. I've continued to get some really amazing business opportunities from Twitter.

Brandon: That is interesting. What have you discovered is unique about Twitter?

Michael: For me, it is a low-stakes environment where people are willing to give you some of their time, you can make connections, and you can easily engage with people. If I call an expert up on the phone and ask for 20 to 30 minutes of their time, that's a high-stakes environment. But if I tweet them and ask them to take a few seconds of their time to reply and click on the link I sent, they will think, "Sure, I can do that."

Brandon: How do you find the time for social media amidst all of the other things you have to do?

Michael: Social media is networking and marketing. I have two choices: I can spend my time networking and attending marketing meetings where I shake hands with 20 people, get three business cards, go to lunch with one of them and possibly close the account months later, or I can take the cumulative time I would spend on those networking opportunities and write an article that thousands of people will see. This will yield a greater return on my investment of time.

As we've talked about throughout this book, content is key when establishing yourself as a thought leader and enhancing your brand. Twitter is a great place to tie together all of your content marketing strategies in a quick and efficient way. There are three ways to use Twitter to your advantage as a financial advisor: field customer service requests and direct traffic back to your blog or other social media platforms.

BY THE NUMBERS

According to the Pew Research Center, of the users on Twitter, **27%** have a household income of over $75,000.[42]

HANG UP THE PHONE AND TWEET

The days of toll-free lines, long wait times, and frustrating conversations are slowly fading away. Instead, more and more companies (like American Airlines, mentioned earlier) are turning to social media to field their customer service requests. According to J.D. Power, 67% of consumers have used a company's social media site for servicing.[43] Social media is quicker and reinforces to your clients and other users that you care about their satisfaction.

As an independent financial advisor, you likely don't have queues of disgruntled customers waiting to talk to someone, but you can still utilize Twitter as a way to connect with your clients and field their concerns. You can start by:

- Setting aside time once a day to respond to your mentions (when people tag you with an @ sign) on Twitter. Don't ignore any negative feedback you receive, but instead provide a solution to their issues or an alternative way to contact your office directly.

- Studying the best practices of corporations on Twitter. How do they field their incoming customer satisfaction tweets? How timely do they respond, and what is the result?

- Asking your customers if they would appreciate the option to reach out to you via Twitter.

USING TWITTER AS A ROAD BACK TO YOUR WEBSITE

Twitter's character limit is both a blessing and a curse, depending on how you use it. If you are looking to Twitter as the platform to publish that blog you have spent months working on, you are going to be sorely disappointed. But if you view Twitter as another road that leads back to your website and to share quick tidbits about your content, you will find it a useful inbound platform.

For example, let's say you recently wrote a blog about the importance of saving for retirement early. You interviewed both a young professional and a person living in retirement and got some great quotes. They live in the blog post, but you quickly tweet them out with a link to the whole story. Users then see the quote, are intrigued and click to learn more, and instantly find themselves on your website. This is a great example of how Twitter can be used wisely.

Another way to use Twitter's short character limit to your advantage is to Tweet about events as they happen. In 2015, as the Department of Labor's fiduciary rule was changing, many advisors took to Twitter to explain, in the simplest terms, what was happening and how it affected their clients. They gave a day-by-day playback of current developments as they happened. This is a great way to use Twitter to stay on top of industry trends.

In addition to the content you post, Twitter is also a crucial part of your visual branding strategy. Before you even start to think of tweets, remember to add your headshot, logo, and cover photo. These images should tie into your website and social media platforms. Fill your bio in with some basic information about you, your focus, and your firm and always link back to your website.

THREE WAYS FINANCIAL ADVISORS CAN ADVERTISE ON TWITTER

Depending on your goals, Twitter offers different ad campaigns that accomplish various things. For example, their website-clicks campaign's goal is to gain website traffic, while the followers campaign's goal is to increase followers on your profile. Here are three advertisement campaign options on Twitter.

1. WEBSITE-CLICKS CAMPAIGN

Like other social profiles, this ad tool is created to increase traffic to your website and motivate an audience to take a specific action. Twitter uses what they call a Website Card, which appears on users' feeds, to grow your site traffic and drive specific actions. A Website Card usually includes an image, a short sentence about your business, and a link to your website.

This campaign is great for advisors who want to direct their followers and prospects back to their site because that is where they offer the most value.

2. FOLLOWERS CAMPAIGN

According to Twitter, 69% of users buy from a business they follow on the platform.[44] Businesses with large social media followings are also often seen as more credible. If you think you have a strong Twitter profile, meaning that you consistently tweet a variety of useful, insightful content, Twitter's followers campaign might be right for you.

This campaign involves placing your profile in the "Who to Follow" sidebar, as well as on users' timelines. Some good reasons to run a followers campaign might also include directing users to your profile to offer an exclusive discount, updates on upcoming services or events, or access to industry research. You can create multiple campaign tweets and see which perform the best.

3. ENGAGEMENT CAMPAIGN

Engagement campaigns' goal is to increase retweets, likes, and mentions, thereby spreading your message to a wider audience. Twitter's engagement campaign promotes your tweets to a large, targeted group of people and enables you to place your best content in front of the audience that matters to you. Although these tweets are still labeled as "promoted," just as the above campaigns are, they act like normal tweets and are able to be liked and retweeted.

Each of these ad campaigns have pros and cons and should be approached differently. For example, tweets are more likely to get higher levels of engagement with photos, but photos may distract from the call to action if you are simply trying to gain more followers. Experiment with the ads offered to decide which are best for your business.

SO MANY SOCIAL MEDIA PLATFORMS, SO LITTLE TIME

I generally shy away from recommending that advisors jump on the hottest social media platforms of the moment because, chances are, most of them will be obsolete by the time you are reading this. That being said, though, we would be remiss if we didn't at least cover some of the main platforms active on the Web today.

Pinterest — I covered Pinterest briefly in the previous version of this book, and it's worth mentioning that it is still a viable platform today. Although not the most sensible choice for financial advisors, Pinterest provides users with the opportunity to "pin," or save ideas they are interested in, such as home design, fashion, and cooking.

Periscope — Periscope is one of the leaders in live video broadcasting, and as live video has gained traction, Periscope has grown. For small businesses owners, this app provides the opportunity to broadcast a live video of something happening, such as the grand opening of a new location or the introduction of a new team member.

Snapchat — Notable magazines such as *Financial Planning* and *Investment News* have done pieces about the rise of Snapchat in the midst of robo-advising. Snapchat is an app that allows users to post short videos or pictures of themselves, but they can only be viewed for up to 24 hours. How an advisor would benefit from these features is still up in the air.

YouTube — YouTube is actually larger than LinkedIn and Twitter and definitely worth looking into as a financial advisor. It has been around a long time and has now introduced a live video option, which broadens the horizons for marketers. If you enjoy making and posting videos, YouTube is the social media platform for you.

Instagram — Instagram is a photo-sharing site owned by Facebook where users post videos and images using filters and hashtags. Instagram has a generally younger user base, which might be beneficial for advisors looking to target Millennials and their colleagues. With over 100 million users,[45] it might be worth the research to see how you can use this growing platform to your advantage.

Now that we have gone through the benefits of Twitter and how it can be of value to your business, now's the time to get started by making yourself a profile.

First, go to Twitter.com and click on "Sign up." You will be prompted to enter your full name, email, and to create a password.

Next, you will choose a username. We suggest a name that relates directly to your business' name or your legal name. Consistency on other social media platforms is important because it reinforces your brand.

Once your profile is established, Twitter will suggest you follow certain people to populate your feed. Some examples may be thought leaders in your industry, direct competitors, clients and prospects, and FMG, of course! You can also upload your email contacts directly into Twitter.

> Treat your social media profiles as extensions of your website and give them the TLC they deserve.

CHAPTER 10:

TAKING SOCIAL MEDIA TO THE NEXT LEVEL

According to a study done by the University of Chicago, more than a third of marriages between 2005 and 2012 began online.[46] The study also found that these couples have happier and longer marriages. The study did not determine why relationships that started online were more successful, but the reasons may include the strong motivations of online daters, the availability of advanced screening, and the sheer volume of opportunities online. Another study shows that the popularity of online dating is no longer limited to Millennials. In the past few years, online dating among 55- to 64-year-olds has risen substantially, having doubled since 2013.[47]

If you would have told me 30 years ago that a person would have had a better chance meeting their spouse through a screen than they would in person, I would not have believed you. But our way of communicating has shifted. Putting your best foot forward online will go a long way, not just in the online dating world, but also when it comes to building your practice. Once you have created your social media profiles and made them look professional, you have to start socializing and taking your strategy to the next level! Brand yourself, target your ideal clientele, engage in conversation, make people feel appreciated, and help them get to know you.

In this chapter, we'll look at a few essential steps to take that will help you maximize your social media marketing and develop a vibrant community that inspires clients and prospects to start talking to you. Just like in the online dating world, people are looking for online business relationships; you just need to find and connect with them. In the end, social media success lies in making personal connections and building relationships to generate new business.

BY THE NUMBERS

As of early 2016, there were **3.17 billion** Internet users, **2.3 billion** of which were also active on social media. On average, Internet users have **5.54 unique social media accounts**, and **91% of brands** use at least two social media channels. [48]

TREAT YOUR SOCIAL MEDIA PROFILES AS A SECOND WEBSITE

Your social media profiles can be used as a marketing and branding tool, just like your website. They contribute to your SEO, help clients, prospects, and referrals find you online, and serve as another resource for people to be introduced to your brand.

Just as you dedicated time to ensure your website reflects your brand through imagery, content, and design, do the same for your social media profiles. Your profile and background photos, about and contact information, and posts should be current and align with the aesthetics of your website. For example, your Facebook and Twitter background photos may be the same photo you use on the homepage of your website, and your LinkedIn headshot the same as the one on your website bio page.

When it comes to setting up their social media profiles, I like to tell advisors to give it 100% or don't create one at all. A profile without an image or with too little information is just as bad as not having a profile at all. For example, without a good head shot, clients may not know if it's actually your profile, so they won't be inclined to like or follow it. And referrals and prospects likely won't trust a mysteriously vacant profile.

TAKE BABY STEPS

To keep your profiles up to date and professional looking, only create as many as you can reasonably manage. Social media takes work, and while much of your content can be shared on all platforms, taking on too many profiles can quickly become overwhelming. It's better to have one or two stellar profiles than three or four mediocre ones.

For financial advisors, I think LinkedIn is the best place to start, as it's catered to professionals, it's the best for connecting with both clients and strategic partners, and its publishing platform is ideal for advisors to establish their expertise and niche.

Once you have LinkedIn under your belt, the next best choice is likely Facebook, simply because of the sheer number of people who are on the network. Facebook and LinkedIn complement one another because you can focus on professional and educational content on your LinkedIn profile, while offering more personal stories, event announcements, and firm updates on Facebook.

If you're feeling particularly social, Twitter is the next platform to join. Twitter is very unique and, therefore, can be difficult to master. It plays by its own rules and depends heavily on quick insights, immediate turnaround, and the latest trends. For example, while most people will wait a day or two for an email response, or several hours for a Facebook or LinkedIn answer, Twitter users expect brands to respond within *one hour.*[49]

I think Twitter is a great social platform for establishing yourself as a thought leader, but it's helpful to have a staff member who can assist with the daily maintenance and communication.

DECIDE ON A DEFINITE FOCUS FOR EACH PLATFORM

The personality, etiquette, and user base for each social media platform is unique, and your focus should match. By featuring different content on different platforms, you can encourage followers to Like and follow all of your channels, rather than just one.

LINKEDIN

As mentioned, LinkedIn is the professional's social network. A study revealed that the social network is the most trusted social platform for financial services companies to engage with high-net-worth investors, and the ultra-affluent (those with $5 million and more in investable assets) are passionate about investment research and rely on LinkedIn as a top resource for this information.[50] LinkedIn is ideal for posting educational articles on financial and investment topics that show you are knowledgeable about your industry.

FACEBOOK

Facebook has established itself as a casual environment with a melting pot of content, from cooking videos to "gifs" to more serious news articles. Use your Facebook Business page as a hub for your daily updates and events. Show your charitable work, personal interests, and even family news items from you and your staff members, as well as events in your community.

Facebook is also a great platform to remind clients and prospects of services they may need at certain times in life. For example, in spring when many students are preparing for graduation, you can remind your followers about the importance of college planning, or how college students can start investing now, even on a limited budget.

CRAIG'S SECRET FOR SUCCESS

Facebook posts with images see **2.3x more** engagement than those without.[51] Make it a habit of asking a team member to be in charge of snapping a few pictures at client appreciation meetings and company events. Search the web for fun illustrations or cartoons that might be humorous or appeal to your clientele. There are many ways you can include images on social media; you just have to get in a habit of incorporating them.

TWITTER

Twitter's quick turnover makes it the ideal channel to comment on and share topical stories. Link to timely articles, quotes, and news reports that inspire your followers to interact with you. Where with Facebook and LinkedIn you can get away with posting once every few days, Twitter demands higher engagement. You can post throughout the day without worrying about overloading your audience with too much information.

Leave the personal posts to Facebook; the long-form articles to LinkedIn; and stick to enticing headlines, quotes, and links for Twitter.

DETERMINING THE IDEAL TIME TO POST ON SOCIAL MEDIA

If there's one marketing topic I see written about consistently over and over again, it's the best times to post on social media. I would love to be able to tell you that posting at noon on a

Tuesday will get you 70% more likes. But the truth is, the best time to post is when the people you want to see your content are online. The best posting times are different for everyone and fluctuate based on your viewers' age, career, geographic location, time of year, and more. To avoid entirely disappointing you, here's what multiple studies agree on as optimal posting times.[52]

Facebook
Saturday and Sunday between 12 and 1 pm
Thursday and Friday between 1 and 4 pm
Wednesday at 3 pm

Twitter
Wednesday at noon or between 5 and 6 pm
Monday through Friday between 12 and 5 pm

LinkedIn
Tuesday between 10 and 11 am
Tuesday, Wednesday, and Thursday between
7:30 and 8:30 am, 12 pm, and between 5 and 6 pm

Time zones can throw a wrench into your plan to match these exact time frames. If you serve clients equally across the United States, you may want to focus on the Eastern time zone, as 50% of the U.S. population is in this time zone.[53]

Your best bet is to make an educated guess, based on what you know about your clients, and then adjust based on your analytics. Post at different times and days of the week and see which posts have the highest engagement levels. Facebook and Twitter make it easy to view past analytics, and you can use separate programs, like Hootsuite or Buffer, to review analytics for all other platforms.

In Chapter 4, we talked about the three types of content to use in your marketing: original, evergreen, and curated. On social media, you'll use a mix of all three, but you want to be discerning in your choices. The goal of social media isn't simply to link to an article you found that might be of interest to your audience. Rather, the objective is to inspire your audience to pause, review, and consider how this information relates to them.

Before sharing a piece of content, make sure it meets the three criteria that make a post successful:

1. **It's Engaging**

   Engaging your connections means giving them a reason to be an active part of your social media efforts. For example, it's been proven that posts with a question receive 100% more comments than standard text-based statement posts.[54] Of these question posts, those with the highest engagement use words such as "should," "would," "which," and "who." The best questions are those that have a limited answer option, as opposed to open question words that require the reader to think more and articulate their answer. When linking to an article, image, or video, think of a question to encourage participation.

2. **It's Informative**

   Six out of every 10 LinkedIn users are interested in industry insights, and it's the most demanded type of content, followed by company news and new products and services.[55] As a financial advisor, your clients want to look to you as a source of information and as a thought leader. Your social pages are the perfect place to show off what you know! Teach them about the market, how to invest, and when to do it.

Some advisors worry about giving away "too much" — like economic insights — on social media. I can see why this is a concern. In the past, when outbound marketing ruled the way we communicated, this might have been valid. But now, things have changed. You are competing against hundreds of free, online, money management tools. If your clients can't see your knowledge up front, they will turn somewhere else to find the information. Content marketing gives you a chance to be the center of your marketing strategy, drawing attention back to you.

3. **It's Entertaining**

   Remember to have some fun! Social media is a great medium to be entertaining, get a laugh, and show that you are different than those online money management sites because you are an actual person! Nothing will emphasize this more than throwing a little personality into your pages.

   Other ways to entertain on social media? Video, video, video! Social video marketing is the way all businesses are moving because they realize how competitive the content space is. Nearly five billion videos are viewed every day online, and the number of people watching YouTube per day is up 40% year-to-year since 2014.[56] It's safe to say that people not only are familiar with watching video on their social sites, but they also expect it. You don't have to make your own videos (though it's certainly a great addition if you have the time and budget). Use evergreen videos from your FMG Suite Content Library and link to ones you find on news sites or YouTube. Videos can be a great balance of education and entertainment.

CREATING A CALENDAR

Whether you're a casual social media user or a marketing maven, a marketing calendar is a must-have organizational tool for independent property and casualty insurance agents, as it helps to define how they will disseminate content and increases the number of referrals and prospects with whom they connect. A marketing calendar helps you:

- Organize, prioritize, and track your marketing initiatives and business goals
- Consistently create, share, and promote quality content
- Cut down on wasted time
- Manage your budget
- Clarify how you will attract prospects
- Define a step-by-step process of what you will accomplish (and how and when)

In Chapter 6, I mentioned the importance of following an editorial calendar. Now, let's address how to create one. A marketing calendar doesn't have to be an elaborate 30-page spreadsheet. You can get started right now and create your schedule for the year in just a few simple steps.

STEP 1: CHOOSE A CALENDAR FORMAT

There are many free ways to develop your marketing calendar. You can create your plan in a Word document or Excel spreadsheet, or write it down with the ever-reliable pen and paper. If you're looking for something more advanced, search online for a marketing calendar service. Some services charge a monthly fee while others allow you to download a free marketing calendar template.

MORE ONLINE

Looking for a great marketing calendar template? We've created one just for you, and it's free! Visit FMG Suite's Resource Center to download yours and watch our broadcast on strategically creating your marketing calendar.

STEP 2: FORMALIZE AND EVALUATE TACTICS
FOR ACCOMPLISHING YOUR GOALS

What exactly do you want to achieve through your marketing? Your answer shouldn't just be "more clients." Define specific objectives that are meant to result in more clients who fit within your target market, whether that's high-net-worth families or businesses. This will determine what type of posts you create and what calls to action you utilize. For example, if you want to build your following, you may offer a giveaway or provide an incentive if your followers share your post. Or, if you want to drive more traffic to your website, link to posts on your site with an enticing offer, such as a free whitepaper.

STEP 3: DETERMINE FREQUENCY

How often will you post on social media? Your marketing calendar will help you stick to a set schedule. While it's great to have big goals, keep your frequency realistic. Start small and increase your frequency further down the road. For the first quarter of the year, plan to send out three posts per week. For the second quarter, increase to six posts per week, and so forth. If you'd like to get more done than you can do yourself, consider asking a coworker to help. Once you set your frequency, add the schedule to your marketing calendar.

STEP 4: DEFINE WHO WILL DO WHAT

Play to your strengths and hire your weaknesses. Do what you are good at and find those who excel where you don't. If you don't have the time to post on social media every day, use an automated content service to post three days per week, and create custom posts two days per week.

STEP 5: ADJUST AS NEEDED

Once you've created and launched your marketing calendar, there is always room for adjustments. Regularly evaluate the performance of your efforts to see what is performing well and what isn't. You can measure these results by seeing how many people Liked, shared, favorited, or retweeted a post, or how much website traffic you received when you posted a new blog. If you don't see results, adjust your strategy or research opportunities to improve. If you discover a particular strategy doesn't align with your target market, eliminate or replace it with a more productive tactic.

BUILDING YOUR TRIBE

One of the dangers of social media marketing is getting too caught up in numbers. Likes, follows, conversions, clicks — it all starts to resemble the numbers on any financial spreadsheet. But the reality is that behind each of those clicks is a person who is trying to solve a problem or looking for an opportunity.

It's important to remember that your metrics are not just numbers. Each engagement represents a touch point in your one-on-one relationship with your prospects and clients. When someone connects with you on social media, they should feel like they are starting a journey with you that will benefit everyone. And if they do, they'll be happy to invite others along.

This is where the concept of tribes comes into play. Marketing guru, Seth Godin, created the idea of tribes within marketing. Tribal marketing refers to targeting a tribe that is your ideal client base and marketing directly to it. These people share the same interests and are supporters of your business. Tribes are digital communities where three things come together: a leader, a common idea, and a way to communicate. Providing all three of these criteria for your clients will not only create a strong digital tribe, but will dramatically grow your business as well.

1. THE LEADER

There's a lot of noise online. A leader who can cut through the garbage and deliver real value stands as out as a high-worth connection. You do this by clarifying your unique service proposition and your big-picture mission, and then sharing that with your clients and prospects. But don't be vague about it.

Clarify your different service features and how they match up with customer needs. Then capture those ideas in articles and tweets.

Decide which tone and language best manifests your personality. Or if you are feeling lost, make an appointment with one of our copywriting strategists. They are great at helping people see the next step to take.

2. THE COMMON IDEA

One of the best ways to make someone feel like they are part of your tribe is to have them invite another member with common opinions. Asking for referrals can seem intimidating, but in fact, it is an opportunity for you to provide an additional service to your clients. They rely on you to take care of their problems if they see you do the same for another.

Having a referral link on your social media profiles and website is a great context for taking role call in your tribe, and this form can be the primary point of initial data collection. If someone wants to know what you have to say, you want to give them the chance to hear you say it.

3. THE COMMUNICATION

One great way to build your tribe is to start a LinkedIn group. Or, if you already have one, start taking it more seriously. LinkedIn groups are continuously brought up by clients and end users as a place they go for in-depth knowledge. The format of them allows you to share insights on topical articles quickly or share original material from your LinkedIn publications. If you keep the group fresh and consistent, it can end up being both a demonstration of your service value and a conduit for new, interested parties to meet you.

Internet users, referrals, prospects, and clients won't just take your word as gold. While your website helps articulate your brand, your social media helps reinforce your message and serves as the hub around which your clients and prospects can unite and confirm your legitimacy. By gathering your supporters together in a digital tribe, you not only create a robust brand presence online, but you also surround yourself with the people you help, and they become a community that you can check in with as often as you like.

> *"A brand is no longer what we tell the consumer it is –*
> *it is what consumers tell each other it is."*
> – Scott Cook, Founder, Intuit

FROM FACETIME TO FACE TIME

Just as every interaction with clients should end with a call to action, your social media should be no exception. Your social media marketing will help you establish and gauge interest. If someone shows a particular interest in a post or has a question, pick up the phone, give them a call and invite them to come in to learn more. Nothing can replace that personal interaction, and only you can make that call.

MAKE IT HAPPEN

Once you have your social media profiles up and running, follow our three tips to strengthen your pages and profiles for maximum reach and interaction.

1. **Respond immediately to all questions or comments**

   When clients make the effort to begin following you on social media, acknowledge them! Thank them when they share a piece of your content or retweet your tweet. Most importantly, answer all comments and questions within 24 hours. If you are worried about keeping up with traffic, set notifications in your settings to send comments to your email inbox. Ignoring comments will discourage your connections to reach out to you.

2. Show your personality

Make your comments and posts personal and warm. When appropriate, disclose personal interests and traits in which your clients might be interested. Allow people a glimpse into your life beyond financial planning.

3. Focus more on relationships than sales

Social media is a place to build relationships; your office is a place to conduct business. Use your social media sites as a forum for conversations, as a place to showcase your unique personality and style, and as a reference center where followers can always find an interesting fact or a thoughtful quote or article. In this relaxed environment, relationships will flourish. Business will inevitably result.

Email is one of the oldest and most effective forms of inbound marketing. How does your email strategy shape up?

CHAPTER 11:

THE NEW EMAIL NEWSLETTER

While my tasks and schedule at FMG Suite differ every day, email is the one thing that's always on my to-do list, and I'm sure it is the same for you. Over the past decade, email has quickly become the favored communication method of both consumers and businesses. It makes it possible for people around the world to communicate at any time of day and share information, whether it's a document or video or image.

Because of its ease of use and omnipresence in our lives, the email marketing platform has vastly grown. Email marketing has been with us now for almost 20 years and, as of 2015, more than 2.6 billion email users are sending 205 billion emails every day.[57] Today, it's one of the top marketing strategies among small and mid-sized businesses largely because of its affordability and return on investment — about a 4,300% ROI. Furthermore, email marketing works 40 times better at acquiring clients than Facebook and Twitter and offers a 17% higher conversion rate.[58]

As email has evolved and its impressive return on investment has increased, its marketing strategies have also changed. Around a decade ago, marketers used the "spray and pray" method, which was sending an advertisement in the form of an email to every single email address they had on file. A few years ago, we shifted to the newsletter, which focused on educational information that directed the recipient back to the sender's website. In the past year, email marketing has evolved yet again and now centers around campaigns.

CAMPAIGNS VERSUS NEWSLETTERS

The email newsletter was one of the early inbound marketing strategies that entered the digital space. Rather than blatantly advertising a service, the newsletter was focused on education. The newsletter was great for financial advisors because it didn't require a lot of time. One single newsletter would be sent to all contacts at once.

While this has proven successful, the rise in automated and behavioral technology platforms led to a reduction of the traditional newsletter approach as email strategies were refined to focus on the specific needs of each contact. The newsletter was a mass inbound marketing strategy; the campaign is a targeted strategy for client communication and branding.

We like to define an email campaign as a strategy where we are sending a steady stream of content, specially formulated for a specific group of clients and prospects, paced at an appropriate rate of time.

With an email newsletter, you likely send one piece of email content to your entire list of contacts. While this is an excellent way to keep in touch with contacts on a regular basis, there's a chance that some of the content you share isn't necessarily applicable to all clients. A campaign is designed to be more strategic and targeted, identifying the unique needs of different groups of contacts and then sending them information that inspires them to take action.

A campaign meets the criterion of "smart email marketing." What makes email marketing "smart" is the adherence to a strategic marketing formula:

1. Raise awareness (informing your contacts about your services)
2. Stimulate a desire for acquisition (telling them how they can achieve what you're providing)
3. Guide the contact toward conversion (transform prospects into clients)
4. Foster customer retention (keep clients returning to you for ongoing services and assistance)

If you're currently relying on email newsletters and have yet to tackle the campaign, fret not. In many ways, email campaigns follow many of the same rules as the newsletter does, but with more insightful strategies behind every message. You don't need to start from scratch; you just need to evolve your current marketing. And if you haven't dipped your toes in the pool of email marketing, now is the time to start.

> *"Email has an ability many channels don't: creating valuable, personal touches – at scale."*
> – David Newman[59]

MAKING THE MOST OF THE PREFERRED COMMUNICATION METHOD

Because of its cost-friendly nature and effectiveness, email has largely become the key communication method between advisors and their clients and prospects. We've previously talked about how the most productive advisors "touch" their clients 12 to 18 times per year. This practice keeps the advisor at the forefront of clients' and prospects' minds so they are more likely to mention the advisor when a referral opportunity arrives. It also improves client satisfaction and increases awareness of other services the advisor offers, resulting in increased business.

And, in today's digital world, it's just good practice to engage frequently with your clients and prospects. People today are conditioned to hear from their meaningful connections regularly. Think about it. Would you return to a blog if it had only posted a new article once a month? Probably not. Would you spend much time on a social media site if it changed every few weeks? Unlikely. For successful communication in the digital age, you must follow three rules:

1. MAINTAINING CONSISTENT FREQUENCY

The first rule for great content for email messaging is frequency. Be a steady voice with clients and prospects. Build a library of enough material so you can communicate with your contacts often. Plan on sending an email campaign at least once a month. If you have the time, you may try to send an article or video once a week. You want to be top-of-mind when people have a question. Don't make them hunt through their inbox when they have a concern. Be a frequent visitor with your emails.

2. OVER-COMMUNICATE

The second rule is related to the first, but applies in particular when the markets become volatile, or fast-moving events cause general concern in the population. You should over-communicate during times like these because the general tendency among advisors is to go silent when times are tough, just when their clients are most in need of reassurance.

For example, if the market falls off a cliff, send something to your clients every day. Time and time again we see studies that say investors complain when their advisor says nothing as the market tumbles lower. For this reason, FMG Suite has content prepared for advisors to send in times of market volatility and you may wish to prepare something in advance for your clients as well.

Imagine how much your clients and prospects would appreciate seeing a video or article about the ups and downs of the investment cycle if the market is trending lower, or how glad they would be to receive an informational piece about tax laws if a major bill is pending in Congress. Conversely, if the market jumps higher due to some good economic news, you may help your clients keep the market's rally in perspective with an article or video on how events influence Wall Street.

3. VARIETY

Consider a combination of content such as a video, infographic, article, or monthly market summary. Variety will make your emails much more interesting and slightly unpredictable. If possible, make it easy for your active clients to forward your emails to a friend and share on social media. That type of smart marketing may generate a lead when you least expect it.

Rather than send the same type of message every week or month, switch up the tone and style. Let's look a little closer at the types of content you can send through your email marketing efforts:

- **Lifestyle**
  Everyone loves lifestyle content, such as "10 Ways to Maximize Your Social Security Benefits" or "5 Signs You're Not Ready for Retirement Yet." These are always engaging pieces that you can create yourself or curate from another source.

- **Market Updates**
  If investing is a significant component of your firm, or you know your clients are interested in the markets, sending a monthly market commentary helps you show your expertise and remind your contacts that you stay up to date on the market so they don't have to. This can be the most challenging content to create, as it's time-consuming and must be completed on a tight schedule, so you might want to use a third-party marketing tool, such as FMG Suite's Campaigns, to save time.

- **Client Events**

  One of the best ways to advertise your upcoming events and boost attendance is to send an invite out via email. Depending on the type of event, you can encourage clients to bring a friend or share the message with their contacts.

- **Firm News**

  Did you add a new team member to your firm? Are you opening up a new office? Did one of your associates welcome a new family member? Some advisors are hesitant to share this type of news, but it's an excellent way to nourish a personal relationship with clients.

Don't assume you're limited to just sharing articles and text-based content in your emails! Visuals, such as infographics and images, and multimedia elements, such as videos, are a great way to boost your results and make your email more engaging.

BY THE NUMBERS

Advisors who communicate personally with their clients 12 or more times a year generate **68% higher revenue** — and far more client loyalty — than those who interact less frequently.[60]

THE EMAIL SUCCESS FORMULA

The "perfect" email is different for every advisor as it depends on your audience and the goal of your email message. And as much as crafting a great email campaign is an art, we can add strategy to that art to achieve better results.

Through research and our own testing with advisors, we've discovered that certain elements are nearly always present in the most successful email campaigns. At FMG Suite, we like to think of this as the advisor's email marketing equation for success.

Here are five rock-solid tips for creating great email campaigns.

1. BUILD ANTICIPATION

One of the keys to getting your emails opened in this competitive marketplace is to build anticipation. If you can get your clients and prospects to look forward to your email communications, your open and click-through rates will soar. Your subject line is the natural place to do this.

The key to getting emails opened is to create an email campaign that pops. For this, you need a "hook," or something that will both compel the reader to investigate further and, if done right, create a click-through for you. Lead your email with a statement about something that is relevant to the reader, like tuition costs for college or having enough money to last through retirement. Your "hook" should have both informational and emotive content.

2. FEATURE CONTENT THAT SURPRISES AND DELIGHTS

Earlier, I mentioned that variety of content was key, and that comes into play here. Whether you're sharing a lifestyle article or an educational video, everything you send in your email campaign should surprise and delight.

By this, I mean it shouldn't be the same information regurgitated over and over again, and it shouldn't be the same content splashed across every major newspaper. The only way to keep your contacts subscribed to your email campaigns and engaged is to offer them something they can't easily find anywhere else. Even if you're sharing a blog article on a major event, putting your own spin on it and adding your opinion makes it unique.

3. TELL A GOOD STORY

It's important to keep your email campaigns from becoming too dry. For example, not many people are going to be consistently interested in the new developments in retirement plans, but it's still important to let them know these things. So the key is to package that information in a story. Tell a story about a couple facing retirement who didn't plan adequately. Have an illustration and make your point with a call to action.

Remember, an email campaign isn't a fill-in-the-blanks exercise. Keep your content compelling by focusing on your recipients' attention spans and the things that interest them most. Do this and your contacts will look forward to your newsletter instead of ignoring it.

4. USE VIDEO FOR MAXIMUM ENGAGEMENT

We've mentioned it before, but it's worth repeating: adding links to video will increase your click-through rate and get you more attention. These days it seems that people can't get enough video, and anytime that you give them an opportunity to watch one, your job of generating a click-through gets a lot easier. Video is a great way of communicating both information and emotion and is also much more likely to be shared than any other type of communication.

5. GIVE PEOPLE A REASON TO COME BACK

Many of you may already know about my love of Costco. They have a great business model I love supporting, and they're fantastic marketers. Every time you visit Costco, there's something new. Whether it's a new food sample or seasonal patio furniture, Costco consistently keeps you coming back to see what's new. Because their selection changes frequently and seasonally, shoppers are encouraged to purchase something before it's gone.

To keep your audience engaged in your emails (and by engaged I mean opening and clicking within your emails), you need to give them a reason. What will they get out of it? How will it benefit them to open up a third, fourth, or fiftieth email from you?

For many advisors, the biggest reason will be timely education. To instill this notion in your email contacts, you must send quality content every single time. Stay consistent and your audience will know what to expect and will be more inclined to read your emails and pass them along to their friends and family.

When in doubt, if you don't have something worth saying, don't say it. While it's important to remain consistent in your sending, you don't want to send something out unless you feel it is of quality and interest to your audience.

> **PRO TIP:**
> *Greg Woodbury, Vice President of Sales at FMG Suite*
>
> Email campaigns are the easiest way to educate your clients and motivate them to take action. Say you have a segment of older clients who are overweight in bonds. Send a targeted newsletter reviewing interest rates from a historical perspective and inviting them to schedule a meeting to review their bond holdings. Clients appreciate this and feel well taken care of as a result.

THREE WAYS TO USE VIDEO IN YOUR EMAIL CAMPAIGNS

If you haven't noticed, I'm a big proponent of using video in your marketing strategies, but particularly for email campaigns. Let me explain why.

Categorization refers to the way our minds segment information as it comes in. As consumers, we've had almost 20 years of email marketing to build categories. When I receive an email, it takes less than a second to categorize it as a marketing campaign and, subsequently, something I'm less likely to open. So what's the solution? We need to build a bridge to a different category. This is where video comes in. Since we've had more than 20 years to place video in categories that are associated with excitement, fun, and entertainment, I am more likely to open a video than a text email.

Here's the thing: if you can get your subscribers to see your email campaigns through the category of video (exciting and fun), they are more likely to consume the content and engage with your business. This is one of the reasons that email campaigns featuring video have at least two to three times the click-through rates of standard emails.

If you want to create more engaging content, try these three techniques for adding videos to your email marketing:

ADD VIDEOS THAT EDUCATE

Using motion-graphic videos in your newsletter is a great way to educate your subscribers on different topics. If motion-graphic videos are done right, they raise interest in a subject and encourage the viewer to look deeper.

FEATURE VIDEOS THAT BUILD TRUST

The best way to add trust is to combine a useful and intelligent message with a personal and professional delivery. When done right, trust is established between the presenter and the viewer. A well done video of you talking about important subjects can be very powerful.

USE VIDEO TO PERSONALIZE AND CONVEY TIMELY, RELEVANT INFORMATION

Video blogging is the perfect tool for this. Instead of sitting down to write a quick blog post about market conditions, turn on your webcam and record a short video about what's going on. This form of communication is more informal, personal, and relevant. It creates the feeling that you're delivering a personal, one-on-one message to every person who receives it.

At the end of the day, the reason you send email messages is so your recipients will engage with you. For greater engagement, help your subscribers break out of the box and see your content as fun, exciting, and entertaining, and use video to build the bridge.

BY THE NUMBERS

Why are we such big proponents of using video in email? Forbes reports that **59%** of executives prefer watching video to reading text, and **65%** have visited a business's website after watching its video.[61] Additionally, visuals are processed **60,000x faster** in the brain than text, and **65%** of the population are visual learners.[62]

It's time to create your first email campaign. In an ideal world, you'd have multiple campaigns regularly sending to different niche audiences. Unless you have an in-house marketing team or are using an automated platform (such as FMG Suite's Campaigns tool) this will be too time-consuming for most financial advisors.

However, if you've yet to enlist the help of anyone, let's look at how you can create an email campaign right now.

Step 1: Define a Goal

The first step is to determine what you want to accomplish with this particular campaign. For this example, let's say you want to reach out to pre-retirees who aren't actively working with you yet and encourage them to start working with you.

Step 2: Segment Your List

You won't be sending a niche campaign to every contact, as you don't want to clutter anyone's inbox. Create a sub-list of your target contacts. In this case, it would be all pre-retirees who aren't actively working with you. If you use a CRM, such as Redtail, this will be easier to do, as you'll hopefully already have every contact's essential information, including age and status (hot lead, cold lead, current client, referral, etc.).

Step 3: Create a Timeline

A campaign typically runs for several months (or even a year) on a consistent schedule. For advisors, I recommend once a month for anywhere between 5 and 12 months. This means you need at least five unique pieces of content to share. Develop a timeline for what you'll send and in what order. For your first email, it may start with an introduction, reminding these prospects who you are. Other pieces in this campaign may include information on 401(k) and IRA rollovers, adjusting your portfolio for your preservation and distribution years, and estate planning.

Step 4: Develop the Content

Whether you create the content yourself, curate from a third party, or use from a content library to which you're currently subscribed, you'll now need to pull the content you want for each email. This may be a mix of videos, infographics, presentations, and articles.

Step 5: Schedule

Depending on your preferences, you may schedule all messages up front to trickle out over the next few months, or you may schedule each one individually every month.

Step 6: Coordinate with Your Other Marketing Efforts

To maximize the results of your email campaigns, coordinate them with your social media messaging and website content. For example, if you share an article in your email, you may also include that on your website's blog and social media profiles.

Step 7: Review Your Results

Depending on the email marketing platform you're using, review your analytics to see who is opening and clicking on your emails. If you notice that specific people are consistently reading your emails, reach out to them by phone and ask them what they thought of your email and whether or not they'd like to discuss further.

Step 8: Repeat

Marketing never stops. When one campaign ends, another should begin. Ideally, you're planning several weeks or even months in advance for your next marketing initiatives.

> Gone are the days of crafting a headline and hoping people respond. Ramp up your email efforts and reap the benefits.

CHAPTER 12:

IMPROVING YOUR EMAIL EFFORTS

New technology, marketing tools, and communication methods appear on the market nearly every month, but email has continued to remain the universal, most widely used platform to conduct business online. Despite the growing importance of social media, email is still at the top of the pyramid. One study shows that 62% of Internet users use social media, but 85% use email.[63]

For financial advisors providing a highly personalized service to individuals, professionals, families, and business owners, email is a must-use marketing strategy. However, it's important to realize that email marketing is only as successful as you are strategic. In 2015, the typical corporate email user sent and received 125 emails a day.[64] And we all tend to immediately delete or skip those that don't immediately pique our interest, either because we don't recognize the sender, the email arrives at too busy a time, or the subject line isn't intriguing enough to click.

In the last chapter, we discussed the creative elements of engaging, lead-generating, and action-inspiring email content. Now, it's time to look at the analytical side of email to get your amazing content read and shared.

TALK THE TALK

OPEN RATES:
How many folks actually open the email you send.

CLICK-THROUGH RATES:
How many recipients open the email, then click a link.

BOUNCE RATES:
The percentage of emails that never reach their intended target. Email bounce rates are influenced by email servers, technology, and even the time of day an email is sent.

SPAM:
Irrelevant email messages sent to a large number of recipients. Emails deemed as SPAM by the email server will filter these emails into the SPAM folder.

LIST SEGMENTATION:
Creating smaller lists from your larger contact list. The purpose of list segmentation is to send relevant content to specific audiences, like a list of individuals nearing retirement or young families saving for their child's college tuition.

BUILDING RELATIONSHIPS THROUGH EMAIL

Email has incredible potential to build stronger connections with clients and prospects on a more personal level than other types of marketing. One reason why it works so well is that it can express vulnerability. For example, if you send out an email advertising your most recent blog post, you can ask for reader feedback (both good and bad). Not only does this feedback help you with future posts, but it also reminds your readers that you care about producing content they enjoy.

Another way vulnerability can play into email marketing is by emailing to apologize for a mistake made. For example, we just got some emails from a content marketing agency apologizing for a mistake they made in their previous email. It was humble, apologetic, and fun. We all make mistakes, and email lets you professionally own up to them.

Another strength of email is that with it you can maintain constant contact. Unlike social or blog posts, which are mainly one-way conversations and single interactions, email can go back and forth between service professionals and their clients for extended contact.

Imagine if you sent out an email asking some of your prospective clients what they would like to achieve financially in the next five years. Someone replies and says that they've been thinking a lot about retirement planning. From there, you go back and forth and eventually schedule a time when they can come in to speak with you. This interaction would probably not take place over social media or another more public platform. Email provides the comfort of a private conversation between two people.

Finally, email allows you to personalize your message in ways you can't on your website or social media. It shouldn't surprise you that customers prefer personalized products and services. This is the driving force behind your business: you have personal interactions every day with your clients and they trust you and your expertise. But how does this personalization translate to email?

Thanks to current technology, you can segment your email lists (which we will dive into shortly) into a variety of categories, such as what step your prospects are in their client journey, their age or location, or the type of product they signed up for when they gave you their email address. You can also use tags to add the individual's first name as an introduction to your email message. These features allow you to send personalized emails to groups of people that address their interests.

BY THE NUMBERS
74% of online consumers get frustrated with websites when content (e.g., offers, ads, promotions) appears that has nothing to do with their interests. So it's no surprise that personalized emails deliver six-times-higher transaction rates.[65]

BUILDING AN ENGAGED EMAIL LIST
You're now well familiar with the possibilities of email marketing. But before you can get new leads and see results from your email marketing campaigns, you need an effective email list. Your email list is the foundation of your entire email marketing strategy. Without a solid one, your campaigns will falter, and your

results will be mediocre at best. By taking the time to build your list strategically with qualified leads — emphasis on the word "qualified" — you can generate incredible results.

With some forethought, you can create a great email list that will have a much better rate of return, just by following a couple of steps.

HAVE A NON-THREATENING ENTRY POINT

Anytime you meet with a new referral, prospect, acquaintance, or potential business partner, ask for their email address. Let them know you'd love to send them some interesting and educational materials. When you host an event or seminar, have a signup list requesting an email address. This is non-threatening, and you will find that the emails you send to this list get shared, increasing your list.

BE DISCERNING

When it comes to your email lists, it's about quality, not quantity. You may have a long list of contacts, but not all of them need to receive every email campaign you send. If 90% of your email list is your family and business associates, you're not going to generate new leads. Focus on adding your clients, prospects, referrals, and leads.

REGULARLY CLEAN HOUSE

Today's email marketing landscape demands clean and accurate email lists. Every 6 to 12 months, clean your email lists. Take a look at your email analytics, including open rates and click-throughs. Which contacts are opening and clicking on your emails? Run through the list and remove contacts who haven't engaged with (opened) your emails in the last six months. Send these contacts a final email that asks them to confirm if they want to continue receiving your emails. If they don't respond, permanently remove them.

ADD OPT-IN FORMS ON YOUR WEBSITE

It's hard to build a list if you don't make it easy (or possible) for people to sign up. Your website should include email newsletter signup forms on every page. Ask for minimal information — just their name and email address. (The more information that form fields require, the fewer form submissions you'll receive.) Advanced website platforms, such as FMG Suite, make it easy to add a simple email signup form for email campaigns. However, if you want to grow your list more aggressively, consider using a third-party program and website plugin.

INCLUDE AN INCENTIVE TO SIGN UP

It's not enough to ask someone to sign up to receive your emails. They need a reason. What will they get out of it? Tips on retirement planning? Informative financial videos? And how will your emails help them? New financial knowledge? Retirement confidence? Within your email form, don't just use "Sign Up" for your button text. Try something more enticing, such as "Gain Financial Knowledge" or "Send Me Financial Planning Tips."

ENCOURAGE FORWARDS

Just as referrals often make the best clients, forwarded recipients can also make for new and engaged email contacts. At the bottom of your emails, include a short blurb asking recipients to forward the email to a friend who may find the information useful. We've seen several advisors find success through this method.

By improving your email lists to include engaged and qualified clients and leads, you have a much better opportunity for building and maintaining business. Start making a few simple changes today and, over time, implement more strategies for building your list. Every few months, evaluate your results to see what is working and what needs improvement.

When it comes to your email list, building it is the first half of the puzzle. The other half is segmenting it into various groups. Segmentation refers to the act of dividing your entire list of contacts into subgroups to target more accurately particular types of people with specific needs.

By segmenting your list, you can send messages with calls to action that your recipients are most likely to engage with and, as a result, see an increase in leads, referrals, and new business. While the average open rate for email campaigns is 22.5%, a study found that proper list segmentation can increase open rates by 20% to 40%, with a subsequent rise in click-through rates.[66] There are many different ways to segment a list, but for financial advisors, here are a few common options to help you get started:

AGE RANGE

Age is one of the more basic ways financial advisors and insurance agents may divide their lists, as age often dictates a client's financial concerns. You can segment based on generations, such as Millennials, Generation X, and Baby Boomers, or by a set range, like 20s–40s, 50s–60s, and 70s+.

GEOGRAPHIC LOCATION

Depending on how you operate, you may choose to divide up your lists based on your contacts' locations. If you frequently host office and community events, you may want to create a local (within driving distance) list and a non-local list. This way, you'll only send event invites to the people you know can attend. Or, if you travel around the country, split up your lists by state or area where you visit.

This makes it easy to make announcements on when you plan on traveling and can meet in-person with clients. Lastly, you can split up lists based on the climate and seasons. For example, for the regions that experience heavy snowfall in winter, you could send out a blog post on winter safety tips. For those in year-round warm-weather areas, you would send something different.

INCOME/ASSETS UNDER MANAGEMENT

Splitting up a list based on a client's income level can work well for advisors who use unique strategies or offer certain services for high-income earners. For example, you may only offer an annual review for anyone with $150k to $500k of investable assets, but provide a bi-annual or quarterly review for those who earn over $500k. Or, you may want to send a frequent market update report to high-net-worth clients, but not those who aren't actively investing or who are just getting started investing.

CLIENT TYPE

When in doubt regarding segmentation, this is the first place to start and the type of segmentation every advisor should at least try. This kind of segmentation is ideal for advisors who work with a broad range of clients. You can segment your list and have subgroups for business owners, families, 401(k) participants, retirees, and clients' children and grandchildren. You likely have a different relationship with each of these individuals and a different end-goal in mind. For business owners, it may be maintaining their retirement plan and working with them until they sell their business. For 401(k) participants, it may be converting them to a financial planning client. For families, it may be gaining introductions to children to maintain generational relationships.

FINANCIAL FOCUS

All of your clients have unique financial goals in mind that you can group together in different lists, be it retiring, building their first portfolio, leaving a legacy, or selling a business. By creating subgroups based on your contacts' financial focus, you can send content and information specifically about these goals. This type of segmentation is ideal for sharing lifestyle blogs and news articles.

RELATIONSHIP

If you want to start sending drip campaigns (a series of emails designed to guide a person through the sales funnel), you'll want to segment your list based on your relationships with your contacts, such as long-term client, new client, prospect, referral, or strategic partner. For long-term clients, your focus may be on maintaining strong relationships and reminding them they can reach out to you with questions. For prospects and referrals, you'll likely focus on explaining how you can help them pursuing their financial goals.

HOBBIES & INTERESTS

If you are a content marketer at heart and enjoy sharing lifestyle content, you can segment your lists based on your contacts' hobbies and interests. If you know a lot of golfers, you may group them together into a list and send them information on upcoming golf events, or tie together the game of golf with investing.

LEVEL OF INTEREST

No one likes to be a nag or an email spammer. If you want to send a frequent newsletter or ongoing email campaigns, consider segmenting your list based on their level on the hot–warm–cold scale. If they're a hot lead (highly interested in your services), you can send them more frequent emails than a cold lead who isn't ready to get started yet.

TEN MINUTES TODAY

Think about your client base and who you want to target. Then jot down the different types of groups into which you could break your contacts. You may find that some contacts fit into multiple groups, whereas others only fall into one. This will help you identify your contacts that best meet your ideal clientele and different ways you can connect with them through your marketing.

ENCOURAGING YOUR CONTACTS TO OPEN YOUR EMAILS

As I mentioned earlier, the average business professional receives nearly 125 emails every day. As you can imagine, around 80% to 90% of those are deleted immediately. Along with the email sender, the subject line plays a huge role in whether or not your email is opened or deleted.

If you've built and segmented your list, you won't have to worry about contacts deleting your email because they don't recognize the sender. The only way your emails can survive a mass exodus is by crafting engaging, relevant, and click-encouraging subject lines.

Here's how you can write better email subject lines and improve your email marketing results:

KEEP IT SHORT

While a desktop inbox shows around 60 characters of an email subject line, a mobile device only shows between 25 and 30. When around 50% of people check their email on mobile devices, you want your emails to be mobile-optimized. Keep your subject lines short and sweet. If you feel the need to make it longer, include the most relevant information at the beginning to avoid it being cut off.

DON'T BE OBNOXIOUS

Pranks are for middle school, and no one enjoys being tricked into reading or opening something. Also known as "clickbait," subject lines like "You won't believe this," or "Make $1 million right now" should be avoided. It sounds like spam and most recipients will immediately trash the email. And while we're talking about obnoxious email practices, don't put words in all caps or use excessive exclamation points and question marks.

WRITE LIKE A HUMAN, NOT A BOT

When you meet with a prospect, do you ever scream, "Free consultation! Request now!" Probably not. If you wouldn't say it in conversation with someone, don't write it in an email. You want to come across as professional and thoughtful. A few alternatives that are more engaging and click-worthy:

- When's the last time you reviewed your investments?
- Is it time to review your financial strategies?
- Improve your financial confidence with a complimentary consultation

INCLUDE A DEADLINE (IF IT APPLIES)

Hosting an event? Create a greater sense of urgency by including a timeframe. Instead of "Register for our Annual Financial Markets Review Bruncheon," consider something along the lines of, "Limited Space Available for our Upcoming Event – Reply Soon."

TELL, DON'T SELL

The pros at MailChimp say it best: "When it comes to email marketing, the best subject lines tell what's inside, and the worst subject lines sell what's inside." Your email isn't an advertisement; it's an informative piece of content.[67] Treat it like one. The point of a subject line is to highlight quickly what your email contains. Set your readers' expectations and explain clearly what your email is about.

MAKE AN OFFER THEY CAN'T REFUSE

Let's face it. Everyone wants and expects something from you when you send an email. This doesn't have to be something tangible, such as an event invite or complimentary service. It could be information, such as an article, video, blog post, or whitepaper. If you're sending a monthly email campaign with educational content, mention that value in the subject line. You can do this two ways. First, you can make a statement or ask a question about the topic you're covering, such as "Is It Time to Retire the 4% Rule?" Second, you can specifically mention what you're providing, such as "Discover the 4% Rule Myth in My Free Whitepaper."

Remember: if there's one thing you take away from this it's that there is no one hard and fast rule. While these tips have proven successful, there will always be some variation depending on your audience and contact list. Don't stick to one method just because you read about it. Take chances, try new techniques, and discover what works best for you.

You now know the main components of effective and successful email campaigns. But how do you gauge your progress and improvement? In the end, it doesn't matter how optimized your emails are if you don't know or understand the results they're producing.

Before sending email campaigns, you should ask yourself one question: What is the goal of this campaign?

Address what you're trying to accomplish with your email marketing, whether it's to grow your email list, generate more referrals from current clients, increase your social media following, or convert existing leads into clients.

Once you decide your goal, you need to know what metrics you'll need to track and review to determine the success of your campaign. While there are dozens of metrics you could analyze for days on end, let's look at a few key metrics you should be reviewing for every campaign.

OPEN RATE

Your open rate and click-through rate are the two most basic email metrics. Your open rate tells you two important things:

1. How persuasive your subject is
2. The quality of your email list

For financial advisors, Constant Contact research shows that 14.5% is a good open rate.[68] If your emails are more than 3% under this, you may need to experiment with your subject line or evaluate your list and whether or not you're sending information in which they're interested.

CLICK-THROUGH RATE

This metric is important because it provides insight into how many of your contacts are engaging with your content and interested in learning more about your services. On average, click-through rates are around half of your open rate. According to that same Constant Contact research, financial advisors see a 7.8% average click-through rate.

If your click-through rate is significantly lower than your open rate, you may have a great subject line, but the content within your email isn't relevant or doesn't feature an enticing call to action. Try experimenting with your email links to encourage more of your contacts to click and read more.

BOUNCE RATE

A high bounce rate can get you blacklisted from some email servers as it shows you may be emailing people you don't know or from whom you have not gained permission to contact. The lower your bounce rate, the better. If your bounce rate is above 5%, it's time to clean your email list and eliminate contacts who are bouncing or who haven't opened an email from you in over six months.

Track and review these three key metrics every month for every campaign you send. The key to tracking is to ask questions. When something doesn't look right, ask why. This will help you figure out what to change to make it better next time. In the end, you can always do better. You might consider tweaking your copy or segmenting your list.

Then, repeat the whole process the next month, the one after, and so on. Repeat what works and toss what doesn't. Don't get in the habit of repeating marketing that doesn't work; it's a waste of money. Let the dust settle before you decide what's working. Small incremental changes are the best way to fine-tune your marketing. If you change too much at one time, you will always be chasing the target. Resist the temptation to make massive changes in one cycle.

CRAIG'S SECRET FOR SUCCESS

The real power of digital marketing is synergy; the sum is always greater than the parts. When it comes to email marketing, your website is just as important as your emails. Why? Because only when you treat your website and email marketing as a single initiative can you maximize the power of both. We call this "closing the digital marketing loop."

For example, you should automatically feature the same content that you send out in the newsletter on your homepage. Use site behavior to segment and target your email list and then use the website to make it simple for newsletter recipients to refer friends. Remember to close the marketing loop and get your tools working together. Don't waste opportunities to engage new clients.

TYING IT ALL TOGETHER: SIMPLE WAYS TO IMMEDIATELY BOOST YOUR EMAIL MARKETING ROI

We've covered a lot in this chapter, and I hope I haven't overwhelmed you too much. Before we wrap up our conversation about email, I want to take a moment to tie together everything we've discussed and look at a few quick and simple ways you can immediately boost your email marketing results and return on investment.

OPTIMIZE FOR MOBILE

Since 53% of emails are opened on a mobile device (and with that number continuing to grow every year), your emails have to be mobile-optimized.[69] In fact, 75% of email subscribers say they are highly likely to delete emails that do not render well on mobile devices. The easiest way to achieve this is using an email campaign platform that automatically makes your email templates and messages mobile-friendly. Even when using a mobile-friendly platform, if you are creating your own messages or designs, test your email and make sure it appears correctly on a mobile device before sending.

PERSONALIZE

Consumers expect unique messaging tailored to them. The most obvious way to personalize is to use your contact's first name in the subject line or body of the email. Segmenting your email lists is another way to personalize your messages in a more sophisticated manner than just adding a name to an email. Create subgroups within your lists based on various demographics, from age and profession to hobbies and geographic location, depending on the content you send or the results you want to achieve.

SURVEY YOUR CONTACTS

Once a year, survey your contacts and clients regarding your email marketing. While this can take some time, the end results are worth the work. Either in meetings with clients or through an email, survey your contacts with questions such as:

- How often do you want to receive emails?
- What type of content would you like to see more or less of?
- What time and day of the week do you prefer to receive emails?
- Do you have any friends or family you think would enjoy receiving these emails?

While statistics and research are helpful, nothing beats cold, hard facts straight from your client base.

ADD IMAGES AND VIDEO

A strong email campaign that gets results doesn't look like your standard email. It should include visual elements, including images and video. A Skyword study found that total views of their content increased by 94% when they included at least one image.[70] Why? Visuals make people stop and think. They consume the image and, if it's good, they then go on to look at the rest of your message. Along with pictures, video is the favored communication method among most Internet users. People are 10 times more likely to engage, embed, share, and comment on video content than other types of content.[71] Furthermore, using the word "video" in your email subject line can boost open rates by 19% and click-through rates by 65%.[72]

PROVIDE VALUE

The easiest way to lose prospects and see an increase in unsubscribe rates is by turning your emails into a sales pitch. The goal and expectations of your email marketing shouldn't be to sell your services. It should be to showcase you as a trusted and knowledgeable professional who can solve people's problems. Your email messages should provide valuable content that alleviates pain points and inspires action. If the content is engaging enough, your readers will pick up the phone or email you for more information. Give 90% of what you know away and encourage people to contact you for the other 10%.

INCLUDE A CALL TO ACTION

If your analytics show that people are opening your emails but not clicking through, it's likely because you lack a compelling (or any) call to action. While your recipient may read your email and find it interesting, if you don't prod them to take the next step, they likely won't, either because they don't know there is a next step or they don't know what the next step is. Every email should include a call to action — preferably a visually engaging button — that encourages readers to take the next step, whether that's reading more content on your website, signing up for your next community event, or contacting you for a consultation.

ADD SOCIAL SHARE BUTTONS

With social media, you can take your email campaigns from a moderate success to viral status. On average, by adding social share buttons, email click-through rates increase by 158% compared to emails without it.[73] Social share buttons should be visibly placed on any content that you are sharing through your email newsletters to allow the recipients to share the content on their social sites. If they click on the LinkedIn icon, it will send a link to your newsletter to all of their LinkedIn followers. You want to make sure the valuable content in your email newsletters is not wasted in any way. These buttons give your email recipients a seamless way to share your content with their friends across their social sites.

MAKE IT HAPPEN ▮▮▮▮▮▮▮▮▮▮▮▮▮▮▮▮▮▮▮▮

For your next email campaign, do one thing differently. Whether that's creating a new sub-list, trying a new subject line, or adding social share buttons, change one piece of your email campaign and see what happens. Compare the open and click-through rates with similar emails you've sent and see what kind of results you get.

CHAPTER 13:

PRESENTATIONS ARE HERE TO STAY

I've always considered myself a strong public speaker. After graduating with a communications degree, I was fascinated with the way people receive and respond to messages. During my career as a financial planner, I held countless presentations and seminars in front of hundreds of attendees. When I transitioned to marketing, I knew that I had to use my talent in a new way.

At FMG Suite, Presentations was one of the first tools we created, moving the traditional slide seminar to an online presentation format. Financial advisors have been marketing themselves throughout their careers in multiple ways, and one of those is through presentations. We knew that this tool would be critical in building an inbound strategy.

Fast forward more than six years later and we have multiple inbound marketing tools available for advisors, but the Presentations tool has remained one of our favorites. Our presentations take an advisor's knowledge and our content into the world. Whether you are meeting with one, with a few, or with many, presenting your experience and brand are key.

PRO TIP:
Presentation and public speaker guru, Garr Reynolds, sums up the core of presentations perfectly: "You must be ruthless in your efforts to simplify — not dumb down — your message to its absolute core."[74]

THE THREE GOALS OF PRESENTATIONS

Unfortunately, the first thing that may come to mind when we hear the word "presentation" is a long session in a stuffy conference room, an hour-long slide deck, and an unenthusiastic speaker droning on. These images are the results of decades of presentations and seminars that followed the same, static formula. When I talk about presentations, though, I see them as a dynamic and variable extension of an advisor's content strategy. Just like other inbound marketing tools, presentations serve to educate your clients, enhance your brand, and show your expertise.

THE EDUCATION EQUATION

Educating clients is usually the first goal when financial advisors turn to presentations. The "old" way of communicating — when a professional in a field stands up and tells viewers what to do — is outdated, but people still crave the information provided. They just now expect it to be provided in a new way.

Today, presentations include inseminating information on mobile devices, on social media, and in person. There is also a circular feedback loop; when clients give feedback on your presentations, listen! You may be the "expert" in your field, but by adapting to client feedback, your presentations will become stronger and more effective.

ENHANCE YOUR BRAND

Every piece of content you write, every meeting with clients you have, and every post you share are chances to further your brand. Presentations are just another way to show your clients who you are and why they should work with you. A great way to do this is to make your presentations as personal as possible. Here are a few ways to add a personal touch to an online presentation:

1. Use Case Studies and Stories

People respond to stories rather than statistics. While speaking, you might tend to tell stories and use personal examples more freely than in an online presentation, but this need not be the case. Use animated or personal case studies to infuse a human touch into your presentation and add interest.

2. Use Humor

Nothing shows your personality quite like a little comedy. There are so many ways to add a little, appropriate humor to a presentation. Take a saying or quote that you like and use an app to turn it into a graphic and add that in. Here are a few examples:

Money is better than poverty, if only for financial reasons.
- Woody Allen

Inflation is when you pay $15 for the $10 haircut you used to get for $5 when you had hair.
- Sam Ewing

The economy depends about as much on economists as the weather does on weather forecasters.
- Jean-Paul Kauffmann

3. Use Real Photos

Today, there is no avoiding selfies, and there's a reason for this — people love to take and look at pictures! If you can illustrate financial points with some clever photographs, you will add a whole new dimension to your online presentations. These are just a few ideas for bringing that personal touch into your online and mobile presentations and furthering your personal brand.

STRUT YOUR STUFF

Let's face it: you do what you do because you're good at

it. Most individuals don't know about the world of personal investing, which is why they turn to professionals like you for help. Presentations are a quick and easy way to show what you know and help people across a variety of platforms. Instead of individuals having to reserve a seat to your seminar weeks in advance and plan their travel logistics, they can turn to their iPad on the couch and hear what you have to say.

By harnessing this mobile-friendly way of communicating, you will show your clients and prospects that you know what you're talking about and that they can trust you and your services.

It's also important to note that no matter what the size of your presentation, you should still view it as an opportunity to further your brand. I like to say that there are three kinds of presentations: One on One, One on a Few, and One on Many.

- **One on One**
  These are personal presentations that you might give on the spur of the moment to an interested prospect. I've heard of advisors giving presentations on a flight, at conferences, and even at the grocery store! A prepared advisor is always ready to give a presentation, and mobile and tablet devices make it easy.

- **One on a Few**
  This could be an organized presentation in your community or office and usually involves fewer than 25 people. This is one of my favorite types of presentations because you can give each attendee a higher level of attention.

- **One on Many**
  This is the type of presentation that comes to mind most often, involving a large area, a large group of attendees, and a larger production cost. These presentations are less common than they were a few years ago, but are still a vital part of an advisor's outreach strategy.

CRAIG'S SECRET FOR SUCCESS

Presenting and hosting broadcasts is a big element of my job. I give a lot of them and my best ones are always those for which I've taken adequate time to prepare. When it comes to presentations, I live by the motto that "prior preparation prevents poor performance." From the early seed of an idea to the final designed slides, I like to review my presentations, think on them and stew for a few days, and come back and review again. Give your presentations enough attention beforehand so you feel confident when it comes time to present. And it never hurts to do a practice run!

LEADING BY EXAMPLE

A few of our clients take full advantage of our Presentations tool and use it to generate new business. Deb Sims of Engaging Women in Wealth, for example, uses presentations to target her niche market. She hosts workshops twice a month in her local community of Rancho Santa Fe, California, where she covers a number of financial and investment topics. She guides her clients through family legacy planning, making sense of their financial statements, and Social Security questions.

Her goal is to inspire, engage, and educate women and she provides attendees with the opportunity to learn more about finance in a friendly, warm environment. This is a great example of how presentations act as an extension of Deb's brand and shows off her expertise in financial planning for women.

Her goal is to inspire, engage, and educate women, and she provides attendees with the opportunity to learn more about finance in a friendly, warm environment. This is a great example of how presentations act as an extension of Deb's brand and show off her expertise in financial planning for women.

Another example of an advisor who uses presentations to their full potential is Jeremy Stanley of CRNA Financial Planning in North Carolina. Jeremy works with Certified Registered Nurse Anesthetists (CRNAs) and uses presentations to educate his target market on their financial concerns. He is a sought-after public speaker because of his experience, industry knowledge, and charisma. He provides presentations in person and online through web-based speaking engagements and lectures. There's a reason why his firm's slogan is "Experience the Knowledge!"

PRESENTATIONS, 21ST CENTURY STYLE

The advent of the Internet has changed the way people expect to receive information, and it is growing harder to draw people out of their homes when so much is available online. Savvy advisors will learn to adapt to social media and will present in new and innovative ways.

In order to do that, we need to expand our vision of what constitutes a "presentation." Numerous studies have shown that the attention span of the consumer has changed dramatically as a result of the Internet and mobile devices. The bottom line is that your presentations must be short, visually entertaining and readily available on mobile and tablet devices. And each must include a definite call to action.

Your presentation can last a minute or two, or up to several minutes, so long as it follows those guidelines. Two ways to ramp up your presentations using current technology is through social media and live video streaming.

PRESENTING ON SOCIAL MEDIA

Social media offers you the ability to present your unique message on multiple platforms from the comfort of your desk. Here are three ways you can use social media as a presentation platform.

1. Get an Audience

You cannot give a presentation if you have no one to present to! Your social connections can easily become your presentation attendees. This seems obvious, but I visit dozens of advisors' social sites each week and am surprised by how many have joined social media and are posting regularly but have yet to invite their contacts to connect with them on LinkedIn, Facebook, or Twitter.

Start by posting a well-prepared presentation on your site and link to it from all of your social platforms. Comment about it on your blog, if you have one. This will begin the process of connecting your social media profiles with your website. Presentations are the key because they offer a reason for clients to visit your site.

Remember, in every conversation with clients and prospects, mention your social media profiles so they'll know that you are actively engaged on social media. If you talk it up, they'll take a look.

2. Make it Worth Watching

Once connected with clients, it's important to offer them valuable content that speaks to their interests. Follow the rules of great presentations: keep it short; make it visually appealing; and have a beginning, middle, and an end, including a call to action.

3. Follow Up

After a client or prospect shows interest in any topic on your social media profiles, go old-school: pick up the phone and start a conversation. It's great to use analytics to watch for likes and shares and monitor which topics are getting the most traction. Analytics give you insight into what steps they are looking to take in their financial future but without follow up, the analytics are useless.

Following these three steps on social media will help you transform your social sites into presentation platforms. Presentations have always been, and will continue to be, a vital way to engage and educate clients. Don't miss the opportunity to adapt to changing presentation platforms.

LIVE VIDEO BROADCASTS

Throughout the past year or so, we have really amped up our live video broadcasts. What were once reserved for Dashboard walkthroughs and customer service tips now serve as great marketing outreach. And we aren't alone. With the rise of various streaming sites like Periscope, Facebook Live, and even YouTube, more business owners are turning to live video as a fresh, new way to market themselves.

THE RISE OF ONLINE VIDEO

In 2005, live television shifted. YouTube was born and, within one year, became one of the fastest-growing sites on the Web, with 65,000 videos uploaded every day, reaching 100 million video views. YouTube certainly didn't invent the idea of live video streaming (and most of the videos didn't claim to be filmed live in one take), but it did significantly contribute to the popularity of online video and the notion of peeking into someone else's life via video, as opposed to writing.

Since YouTube, we've seen the expansion into actual live video streaming platforms. Arguably, the first video livestream platform is the aptly named Livestream, which launched in 2007. Today, there are dozens of platforms, such as DaCast, Upstream, Bambuser, and Showcaster.

MORE ONLINE
Check out our archive of past Live Video Broadcasts at
http://www.fmgsuite.com/marketing-broadcasts-archive/.
One of the benefits of live video is that although it is live at the
time, most platforms allow you to archive the video for later use.

LIVE VIDEO STREAMING GETS SOCIAL

Beyond these professional platforms, social media sites have launched amateur-turned-professional live streaming platforms. In 2015, Periscope, a live video streaming app, was developed and acquired by Twitter before it even launched. When airing a live video, Periscope users can tweet out a link to their Live Stream to attain viewers. They can also choose whether or not to make their video public, or they can make it visible only to select users. This is a great option if, say, a financial advisor wanted to host a live video presentation to clients who didn't live locally, but didn't want any outside viewers seeing. The popular photo social network site, Instagram, also introduced the ability to upload video clips in 2013. These clips were limited to 15 seconds until early 2016 when the limit increased to 60 seconds.

Another popular video app is Snapchat, which has more than 100 million daily users. Similar to Instagram, you can post images and short videos. But more interesting are the newest conversations surrounding Snapchat, Robo Advisors, and financial advice. Snapchat is looking to expand into a Robo Advisor platform, like Betterment, using algorithms to manage users' money using ETFs and similar low-cost diversified investments. Whether or not it makes sense for a social media platform to enter into investing is a whole other argument, but one we should be keeping an eye on.

And the latest to enter the live streaming world is Facebook with Facebook Live. Facebook Live allows users to stream live video, invite friends and followers to watch, send out early notifications, and allow viewers to interact in real time. Facebook

Live is one of the more impressive streaming platforms via social media because it's easy to use and can make the biggest impact.

INCORPORATING LIVE VIDEO STREAMING INTO YOUR MARKETING

The question now is: Should advisors be using live video streaming in their marketing? I've already shared the importance and impact of video marketing at some length. So, in the simplest of answers, yes, video is worth using in your marketing.

However, live video starring yourself isn't for everyone. If you're willing to give it a try, start making a few short videos using Periscope and only inviting your closest clients and family members. It will be less intimidating for you knowing that only a handful of people are watching. From there, you can slowly build up to hosting more live videos and eventually open them up to the public. These live videos are essentially online presentations.

Can't imagine yourself in front of a camera? Don't force yourself. Nerves show on camera, and there's no need to put yourself in an uncomfortable position. Instead, stick to other forms of video marketing, such as utilizing educational videos on financial topics that you can share via social media, email, on your website, and in presentations.

MAKE IT HAPPEN ▰▰▰▰▰▰▰▰▰▰▰▰▰▰

Think about the most frequent conversation that you have with prospects. Whether it be the cycle of investing, the importance of diversification, or the concept of compound interest, take some time to discover how you could present that conversation more powerfully to engage and motivate clients. Research which charts, illustrations, and videos exist on the concept and how you could put them together to weave a great story. Save your presentation somewhere easy to access on your mobile device and use it the next time you're meeting with a prospect.

> There's no stopping the evolving nature of marketing, but that doesn't have to be a bad thing if you know how to harness it.

CONCLUSION:

THE POWER OF PERSISTENCE

I've been involved in marketing for more than 30 years, and I'm still learning something new every day. For financial advisors, it's much the same in their industry. They're constantly learning about new strategies, technology, and trends and, in order to stay up to date, they're improving their tactics and sharpening their skills.

This is just one of the reasons why I firmly believe that as a successful financial advisor, you have already been a great inbound marketer for years. You just may not realize it, or know how to use it strategically to your advantage. The foundation of inbound marketing is education, knowledge, and communication — three key characteristics of successful financial advisors. By focusing on integrating these elements into your marketing and client relationships, you'll see your business flourish.

EDUCATION AND KNOWLEDGE

Your clients and prospects must be able to trust that you know what you are doing when you recommend investments. All that we have said about offering tidbits of valuable information to your clients helps build this trust. In addition, online presentations, articles, and other informative materials your clients receive through your website and social media sites will help build that foundation of trust in your competence and provide ongoing education.

Your clients want to see a wide range of topics covered on your website and social sites, whether or not they have a specific need to learn about that topic. Mix it up to help build clients' confidence in your competence.

COMMUNICATION

The most common complaint about financial advisors from clients is not the quality of their advice, but the quality of their client communication. Two aspects of communication are key here: managing client expectations and maintaining a constant line of communication in times of uncertainty. It is easy to think that experienced investors understand risk and the volatility of the markets. But the last major financial crisis showed us that anyone can be caught by surprise! Market uncertainty should be a part of every discussion.

THE ESSENCE OF INBOUND MARKETING

We've talked a lot about marketing throughout this book, but if you asked me to sum up inbound marketing in one phrase, I would say it's about sending the right content to the right people at the right time.

I realize that this is easier said than done, but no one has ever accused marketing of being easy. At FMG Suite, we aim to capture this essence by using the feedback loop. A feedback loop is a three-step repeated system — build, measure, learn (and repeat, repeat, repeat). This is a great way to continuously improve how you work, what you offer, and how you communicate your offering. The more you know about what your clientele likes, wants, and responds to, you'll know what kind of content to send to a specific group of people at a time that makes sense in their lives.

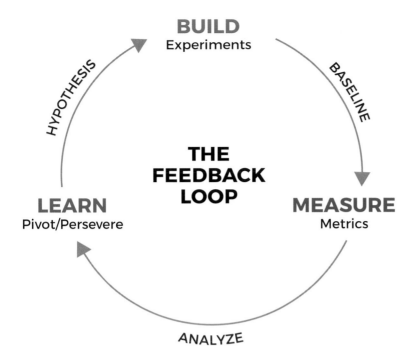

BUILD
Experiments

HYPOTHESIS

BASELINE

THE
FEEDBACK
LOOP

MEASURE
Metrics

LEARN
Pivot/Persevere

ANALYZE

At FMG Suite we don't just recommend the feedback loop to advisors, we use it ourselves. The feedback loop has helped us make immense improvements to our marketing platform, including introducing new tools and adding features advisors told us they wanted. This has significantly contributed to the company's growth.

Marketing can seem overwhelming for many advisors, but don't let procrastination or fear hold you back. With every new task, we all start at step one. You can't progress to steps 3 or 10 or 20 without starting at the beginning. Start small, launching one marketing tactic at a time. As Ralph Waldo Emerson once said, "That which we persist in doing becomes easier to do, not that the nature of the thing has changed but that our power to do has increased."

The more effort you put into marketing, the more rewards you reap. As challenging as marketing can seem at times, successful businesses have proven time and again that the results are worth the work. I encourage you to dive in right here, right now and do one thing differently with your marketing. It can be as small as changing an image on your website or as large as creating a new email campaign. Whatever you choose, hone your marketing chops, measure the results, learn from them, and make adjustments. Be persistent, dare to take risks, and have some fun!

MAKE IT HAPPEN

Drop me a line! Just as I've encouraged you to open the lines of communication with your clients, I hope you will take a minute and let me know what has worked well for you in your own digital marketing efforts. We are continually amazed at the creativity and ingenuity of professionals around the country, many of whose experiences we have shared in these pages. We want to hear from you! Share your own secrets for success by emailing me at marketing@fmgsuite.com.

NOTES

1. Fry, Richard. "Millennials Overtake Baby Boomers as America's Largest Generation." Pew Research Center. April 25, 2016. http://www.pewresearch. org/fact-tank/2016/04/25/millennials-overtake-baby-boomers/

2. "The 'Greater' Wealth Transfer." Accenture. June 2012. https://www.accenture. com/us-en/~/media/Accenture/Conversion-Assets/DotCom/Documents/ Global/PDF/Industries_5/Accenture-CM-AWAMS-Wealth-Transfer-Final-June2012-Web-Version.pdf

3. Tuohy, Cyril. "Tech Can Be the Make-Or-Break Issue." InsuranceNews.net. May 7, 2014. http://insurancenewsnet.com/innarticle/Tech-Can-Be-The-Make-Or-Break-Issue-a-500355

4. Morrissey, Bill. "How Brokers Can Navigate Consolidation in the B-D Industry." Investment News. February 4, 2016. http://www.investmentnews. com/article/20160204/BLOG09/160209951/how-brokers-can-navigate-consolidation-in-the-b-d-industry

5. "Personal Financial Advisors." United States Department of Labor, Bureau of Labor Statistics. http://www.bls.gov/ooh/business-and-financial/personal-financial-advisors.htm

6. Malito, Alessandra. "Too Many Robos Crowding the Market?" Investment News. February 8, 2016. http://www.investmentnews.com/article/20160208/ FREE/160209927/too-many-robos-crowding-the-market

7. McGrail, Mike. "The Blogconomy: Blogging Stats [INFOGRAPHIC]." Social Media Today. August 28, 2013. http://www.socialmediatoday.com/content/ blogconomy-blogging-stats-infographic

8. Rainie, Lee, Sara Kiesler, Ruogu Kang and Mary Madden. "Anonymity, Privacy, and Security Online." Pew Research Center. September 5, 2013. http://www. pewinternet.org/2013/09/05/anonymity-privacy-and-security-online/

9. Lum, Ron. "Survey Says: People Don't Trust Companies with Crappy Websites." Ron Lum. April 19, 2013. http://www.ronswebsite.com/blog/people-dont-trust-companies-with-crappy-websites/

10. Sullivan, John. "6 Things Wealthy Clients Expect of Advisors: IMCA Conference." ThinkAdvisor. April 23, 2012. http://www.thinkadvisor. com/2012/04/23/6-things-wealthy-clients-expect-of-advisors-imca-c?slreturn=1467402920

11. Lynch, J. "U.S. Adults Consume an Entire Hour More of Media Per Day Than They Did Just Last Year." AdWeek. June 27, 2016. http://www.adweek.com/news/television/us-adults-consume-entire-hour-more-media-day-they-did-just-last-year-172218

12. Brosseau, D. "What Is a Thought Leader? FAQ." Thought Leadership Lab. http://www.thoughtleadershiplab.com/Resources/WhatIsaThoughtLeader

13. Nite, Joshua. "Michael Brenner's Tips, Tools, and Templates to Build Your Content Marketing Strategy." TopRank Marketing Blog. September 2015. http://www.toprankblog.com/2015/09/michael-brenner-cmworld/

14. "Marketing Campaign." Entrepreneur. https://www.entrepreneur.com/encyclopedia/marketing-campaign

15. National Client Email Report. Report. 2013. Accessed July 6, 2016. https://dma.org.uk/uploads/National%20Client%20Email%20Report%202013_53fdd7e6684de.pdf

16. Customer Marketing: Improving Customer Satisfaction & Revenue. Report. October 2014. Accessed July 6, 2016. https://blog.demandmetric.com/wp-content/uploads/2014/09/Customer-Marketing-Benchmark-Report.pdf

17. Abramovich, Giselle. "15 Mind-Blowing Stats About Content Marketing." CMO. July 24, 2015. http://www.cmo.com/features/articles/2015/7/22/15-mind-blowing-stats-about-content-marketing.html

18. Nolan, Paul. "Mapping The Buyer's Journey." Sales & Marketing Management. March 27, 2015. https://salesandmarketing.com/content/mapping-buyer%E2%80%99s-journey

19. Gerard, Michael. "Content Marketing Statistics: The Ultimate List." Content Marketing Forum. March 8, 2016. http://www.curata.com/blog/content-marketing-statistics-the-ultimate-list/

20. Miller, Jason. "55 Quotes to Inspire Content Marketing Greatness." LinkedIn. March 28, 2016. https://business.linkedin.com/marketing-solutions/blog/best-practices--content-marketing/2016/55-quotes-to-inspire-content-marketing-greatness

21. Scott, David Meerman. "The New Rules of Marketing & PR." Wiley: New York, 2013.

22. "The State of Content: Expectations on the Rise." Adobe. October 2015. http://wwwimages.adobe.com/content/dam/Adobe/en/max/2015/pdfs/state-of-content-oct.pdf

23. "Over 80 Percent of Financial Advisors Use Social Media for Business According to a 2015 Putnam Investments Social Advisor Study." Putnam Investments.

September 16, 2015. https://www.putnam.com/about-putnam/press-releases/over-80-percent-of-financial-advisors-use-social-media-for-business-according-to-2015-putnam-investments-social-advisor-study.jsp

24. Nason, Deborah. "Want More Clients? Use These Social Media Strategies." CNBC. March 2, 2015. http://www.cnbc.com/2015/03/02/want-more-clients-use-these-social-media-strategies.html

25. "Percentage of U.S. Population with a Social Network Profile from 2008 to 2016." Statista. 2016. http://www.statista.com/statistics/273476/percentage-of-us-population-with-a-social-network-profile/

26. Madden, Mary and Kathryn Zickuhr. "65% of Online Adults Use Social Networking Sites." Pew Research Center. August 26, 2011. http://www.pewinternet.org/2011/08/26/65-of-online-adults-use-social-networking-sites/

27. "Social Media Usage Among Wealthy Investors." Spectrum Group. http://spectrem.com/Content/Social-Media-Usage-Among-Wealthy-Investors.aspx

28. Kim, Larry. "The Best Social Media Networks for Marketers in 2015." Inc. July 13, 2015. http://www.inc.com/larry-kim/the-best-social-media-networks-for-marketers-in-2015.html

29. Duggan, Maeve, Nicole Ellison, Cliff Lampe, Amanda Lenhart, and Mary Madden. "Demographics of Key Social Networking Platforms." Pew Research Center. January 9, 2015. http://www.pewinternet.org/2015/01/09/demographics-of-key-social-networking-platforms-2/

30. Stelzner, Michael. "2015 Social Media Marketing Industry Report." Social Media Examiner. May 2015. https://www.socialmediaexaminer.com/SocialMediaMarketingIndustryReport2015.pdf

31. Smith, C. "125 Amazing LinkedIn Statistics & Facts." Expanded Ramblings. 2014. http://expandedramblings.com/index.php/by-the-numbers-a-few-important-linkedin-stats/6/

32. Abramovich, G. "15 Mind-Blowing Stats About LinkedIn." CMO by Adobe. November 6, 2013. http://www.cmo.com/features/articles/2013/11/4/15_Stats_LinkedIn.html

33. Smith, C. "125 Amazing LinkedIn Statistics & Facts." Expanded Ramblings. 2014. http://expandedramblings.com/index.php/by-the-numbers-a-few-important-linkedin-stats/6/

34. "15 Tips For Compelling Company Updates." LinkedIn. https://business.linkedin.com/content/dam/business/marketing-solutions/global/en_US/site/subsites/content-marketing/pdf/linkedin-15-tips-company-updates-infographic_us_en_130612.pdf

35. Lee, K. "7 Key LinkedIn Stats: When to Post, What to Post & How to Improve." Buffer. 2014. https://blog.bufferapp.com/7-vital-statistics-to-help-with-your-linkedin-marketing-strategy

36. "Top 20 Facebook Statistics." Zephoria Digital Marketing. 2016. https://zephoria.com/top-15-valuable-facebook-statistics/

37. Duggan, Maeve, Nicole Ellison, Cliff Lampe, Amanda Lenhart, and Mary Madden. "Demographics of Key Social Networking Platforms." Pew Research Center. January 9, 2015. http://www.pewinternet.org/2015/01/09/demographics-of-key-social-networking-platforms-2/

38. Ross, Phillip. "Native Facebook Videos Get More Reach Than Any Other Type of Post." Social Bakers. February 17, 2015. http://www.socialbakers.com/blog/2367-native-facebook-videos-get-more-reach-than-any-other-type-of-post

39. Cooper, Belle Beth. "7 Powerful Facebook Statistics You Should Know About." Fast Company. December 3, 2013. http://www.fastcompany.com/3022301/work-smart/7-powerful-facebook-statistics-you-should-know-about

40. "6 Types of Visual Content You Need to Use in Your Marketing Campaigns." Kissmetrics. August 2015. https://blog.kissmetrics.com/visual-content-you-need-to-use-in-your-marketing-campaign/

41. "4 Social Media Trends You Need to Know Going into 2016." Brafton. December 16, 2015. http://www.brafton.com/news/social-media-news/4-social-trends-you-need-to-know-going-into-2016/

42. Duggan, Maeve, Nicole B. Ellison, Cliff Lampe, Amanda Lenhart, and Mary Madden. "Demographics of Key Social Networking Platforms." Pew Research Center. January 09, 2015. http://www.pewinternet.org/2015/01/09/demographics-of-key-social-networking-platforms-2/

43. Perlman, J. "2013 Social Media Benchmark Study." J.D. Power. February 14, 2013. http://www.jdpower.com/press-releases/2013-social-media-benchmark-study

44. "Increase Your Twitter Followers." Twitter. https://business.twitter.com/en/advertising/campaign-types/increase-twitter-followers.html

45. "Top 15 Most Popular Social Networking Sites." eBiz MBA. August 2016. http://www.ebizmba.com/articles/social-networking-websites

46. Jayson, Sharon. "Study: More Than a Third of New Marriages Start Online." USA Today. June 3, 2013. http://www.usatoday.com/story/news/nation/2013/06/03/online-dating-marriage/2377961/

47. Smith, Aaron and Monica Anderson. "5 Facts About Online Dating." Pew Research Center. February 29, 2016. http://www.pewresearch.org/fact-

tank/2016/02/29/5-facts-about-online-dating/

48. Smith, Kit. "Marketing: 96 Amazing Social Media Statistics and Facts for 2016." March 7, 2016. https://www.brandwatch.com/2016/03/96-amazing-social-media-statistics-and-facts-for-2016/

49. Vermeren, Iris. "Marketing: How to Provide Great Customer Service Via Social." Brand Watch. February 25, 2015. https://www.brandwatch.com/2015/02/marketing-provide-great-customer-service-via-social/

50. Savio, Chris and Jake Raroque. "Social Media's Growing Influence Among High Net Worth Investors." LinkedIn. May 2012. https://business.linkedin.com/content/dam/business/marketing-solutions/global/en_US/site/pdf/cs/linkedin_hnw_investor_research_us_en_130314.pdf

51. Mawhinney, Jesse. "37 Visual Content Marketing Statistics You Should Know in 2016." Hubspot. January 13, 2016. http://blog.hubspot.com/marketing/visual-content-marketing-strategy#sm.00000ozlt4817cwkr5u1vpagurtui

52. Ellering, Nathan. "What 16 Studies Say About the Best Times to Post on Social Media." CoSchedule. April 13, 2016. http://coschedule.com/blog/best-times-to-post-on-social-media/

53. "The Science of Social Timing." Kissmetrics. June 2011. https://blog.kissmetrics.com/wp-content/uploads/2011/06/science-of-social-timing-part-1.pdf

54. Cooper, Belle Beth. "7 Powerful Facebook Statistics You Should Know About." Fast Company. December 2, 2013. http://www.fastcompany.com/3022301/work-smart/7-powerful-facebook-statistics-you-should-know-about

55. Lee, Kevan. "7 Essential LinkedIn Marketing Stats: When to Post, What to Post and How to Improve." Buffer. March 24, 2014. https://blog.bufferapp.com/7-vital-statistics-to-help-with-your-linkedin-marketing-strategy

56. "Statistics." YouTube. https://www.youtube.com/yt/press/statistics.html

57. "Email Statistics Report, 2015-2019." The Radicati Group. 2015. http://www.radicati.com/wp/wp-content/uploads/2015/02/Email-Statistics-Report-2015-2019-Executive-Summary.pdf

58. Agius, Aaron. "7 Statistics That Prove Email Marketing Isn't Dead." Entrepreneur. October 22, 2015. https://www.entrepreneur.com/article/251752

59. White, Matthew. "5 Email Marketing Quotes You Need to Hear." Jolt CMS. June 17, 2016. http://www.joltcms.com/5-email-marketing-quotes/

60. "What Do Clients Really Think?" Cetera. February 2013. http://www.fa-mag.com/userfiles/stories/whitepapers/2013/WhatDoClientsThink.pdf

61. "Video in the C-Suite: Executives Embrace the Non-Text Web." Forbes. 2010. http://images.forbes.com/forbesinsights/StudyPDFs/Video_in_the_CSuite.pdf

62. Gutierrez, Karla. "Studies Confirm the Power of Visuals in eLearning." Shift. July 8, 2014. http://info.shiftelearning.com/blog/bid/350326/Studies-Confirm-the-Power-of-Visuals-in-eLearning

63. "Interconnected World: Communication & Social Networking." Ipsos. March 27, 2012. http://www.ipsos-na.com/news-polls/pressrelease.aspx?id=5564

64. Radicati, Sara. "Email Statistics Report, 2011-2015." The Radicati Group, Inc. 2015. http://www.radicati.com/wp/wp-content/uploads/2011/05/Email-Statistics-Report-2011-2015-Executive-Summary.pdf

65. Abramovich, Giselle. "15 Mind-Blowing Stats About Personalization." CMO. February 20, 2015. http://www.cmo.com/features/articles/2015/2/18/mind-blowing-stats-personalization.html#gs.ddUrZPk

66. "Email Segmentation." Marketing Sherpa. April 7, 2015. http://www.marketingsherpa.com/article/case-study/email-segmentation-open-rate-increase

67. Gardner, Oli. "How to Write the Perfect Email Subject Line [Infographic]." Unbounce. January 23, 2013. http://unbounce.com/email-marketing/perfect-subject-line/

68. "The Average Open, Click-Through, and Bounce Rates of Other Constant Contact Customers by Industry." Constant Contact. May 2016. http://support2.constantcontact.com/articles/FAQ/2499

69. "The New Rules of Email Marketing." Campaign Monitor. https://www.campaignmonitor.com/resources/guides/email-marketing-new-rules/

70. Gonsalves, Caleb. "Skyword Study: Add Images to Improve Content Performance." Skyword. August 31, 2012. http://www.skyword.com/contentstandard/marketing/skyword-study-add-images-to-improve-content-performance/

71. Ciampa, Rob. "Video Content Marketing: 4 Elements of An Effective Strategy." Content Marketing Institute. March 22, 2013. http://contentmarketinginstitute.com/2013/03/video-content-marketing-effective-strategy/

72. Mawhinney, Jesse. "37 Visual Content Marketing Statistics You Should Know in 2016." Hubspot. January 13, 2016. http://blog.hubspot.com/marketing/visual-content-marketing-strategy#sm.00000ozlt4817cwkr5u1vpagurtui

73. "20 Marketing Stats on the Trends of 2015." Nonprofit Hub. http://nonprofithub.org/nonprofit-marketing-plan/20-marketing-stats-trends-2015/

74. Reynolds, Garr. "Make Your Presentations Stickier: These 3 Books Can Help." Presentation Zen. July 28, 2007. http://www.presentationzen.com/presentationzen/2007/07/make.html